CARFIT

Englisch für Kfz-Berufe
Lehr-/Arbeitsbuch

Wolfram Büchel
Cornelius Carey

Ernst Klett Verlag
Stuttgart · Düsseldorf · Leipzig

Reihe »Bausteine Englisch für Berufliche Schulen«

CARFIT

Englisch für Kfz-Berufe
Lehr- / Arbeitsbuch

Wolfram Büchel
Cornelius Carey

Many thanks to the teachers who piloted this book and made valuable contributions.

Werkübersicht

Lehr- / Arbeitsbuch	3-12-808310-x
Kassette	3-12-808311-8
CD	3-12-808312-6
Lehrerhandbuch	3-12-808313-4

1. Auflage 1 6 5 4 | 2008

Alle Drucke dieser Auflage können im Unterricht nebeneinander benutzt werden. Die letzte Zahl bezeichnet das Jahr dieses Druckes.

Internetadresse: http://www.klett.de

Redaktion: Inge Spaughton

Technische Beratung: Nicolai Kästle

Einbandgestaltung: Elmar Feuerbach

Druck: W. Wirtz, Speyer. Printed in Germany

ISBN 3-12-808310-x

Inhalt

Vorwort

Globalisierung und internationale Zusammenarbeit in Wirtschaft und Technik haben die Kommunikationsfähigkeit in der Fremdsprache Englisch längst zu einem wichtigen Einstellungskriterium in Industrie und Handel gemacht. Daher wird der Förderung und Vertiefung der Fremdsprache in der Berufswelt immer mehr Beachtung geschenkt. Die wachsenden internationalen Verflechtungen werden kaum irgendwo deutlicher als in der Kfz-Industrie mit Zulieferern aus aller Welt und Produktionsstätten rund um den Globus. Junge Fachkräfte in der Autoindustrie werden daher immer häufiger mit der Fremdsprache Englisch konfrontiert, sei es durch englische Betriebsanleitungen oder englischsprachige Kunden und Lieferanten.

CarFit berücksichtigt die sich verändernde Arbeitswelt und spricht gezielt Auszubildende in Kfz-Berufen an, die am Berufsschul- oder Fachschulunterricht oder an betrieblichen Fortbildungsmaßnahmen teilnehmen.
Das Lehrwerk setzt Grundkenntnisse des Englischen auf dem Niveau des Hauptschulabschlusses voraus.

CarFit vermittelt praxisnahe Fremdsprachenkenntnisse, deren Themen durch Lehrpläne für den praktischen und theoretischen Unterricht vorgegeben sind: Werkzeuge und Maschinen und deren Handhabung, praktische Grundkenntnisse und Fertigkeiten, Arbeitsvorgänge und natürlich die entsprechenden Sicherheitsbestimmungen. Ergänzt werden diese Themen durch kommunikative Fertigkeiten wie Kundengespräche, Telefonieren, Verfassen von einfachen Geschäftsbriefen und E-Mails.

CarFit ist als **Lehr-/Arbeitsbuch** (Verbrauchsmaterial) konzipiert. Zwölf übersichtliche Units mit jeweils vier Seiten bestehen aus:
- einer motivierenden Auftaktseite mit Einführung in das Unit-Thema
- einer Doppelseite mit **themenbezogenen Texten und Übungen**
- einem **Spot on grammar** mit grammatischen Übungen, sowie (wenn zum Thema passend)
- einem **Spot on safety** mit Sicherheitshinweisen

CarFit bietet außerdem **Hörverstehensaufgaben** unterschiedlichster Art. Das Symbol kennzeichnet jeweils die Teile, zu denen Tonaufnahmen auf **Kassette oder CD** vorliegen. Die Hörverstehenstexte sind im Anhang abgedruckt.
Das Symbol kennzeichnet Teile, die außerhalb des Buches schriftlich bearbeitet werden.
Dieses Symbol wird bei Partner- oder Gruppenarbeit bzw. beim Role play verwendet; die Lehrkraft kann hier ein Zeitlimit für die Bearbeitung dieser Aufgabe setzen.

Neue Vokabeln erscheinen kursiv im Text und im Vokabelkasten auf jeder Seite.
Im Anhang befinden sich u. a.
- die **alphabetische Wortliste** mit Lautschrift und Erstvorkommen
- ein technischer **Fachwortschatz *deutsch – englisch***
- die wichtigsten **unregelmäßigen Verben**
- alle **Hörverstehenstexte**

Als Besonderheit bietet *CarFit* eine **gezielte Vorbereitung auf die KMK-Zertifikatsprüfung Englisch Niveaustufe 1** an: in den Units sind entsprechende Aufgabentypen wie ***Reception, Mediation, Production*** und ***Interaction*** eingearbeitet. Im Lehrerhandbuch werden diese Aufgabentypen in zwei Übungsklausuren zur KMK-Prüfung Niveaustufe 1 angeboten.

Der Schlüssel zu allen Übungen im Lehr-/Arbeitsbuch ist im Lehrerhandbuch zu *CarFit* abgedruckt.

Viel Spaß und Erfolg bei der Arbeit mit diesem Buch wünschen Ihnen
Autoren und Redaktion

UNIT 1

The general workshop

The job of a car mechanic today *involves* special fields such as *manufacture* and *assembly* of the car body and the engine. *Trainees* in their first year of training also learn some of the basics of *mechanical engineering*. That is why they have to know the hand tools, *power tools* and *machine tools* that are often used in a general workshop.

A Match the following tools with the illustrations below.

1. screwdrivers
2. *combination pliers*
3. *spanner*
4. *square*
5. *column drill*
6. *vice / bench vice*
7. *hacksaw*
8. *angle grinder*
9. *adjustable wrench*
10. file

a. ☐

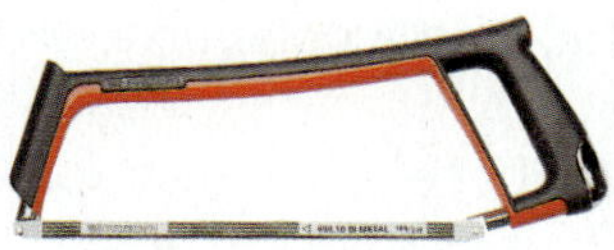

b. ☐

c. ☐

d. ☐

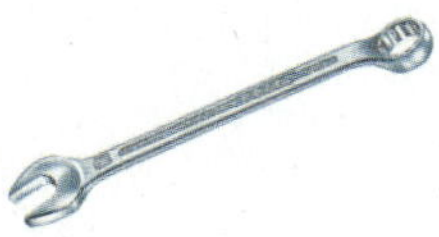

e. ☐

f. ☐

g. ☐

h. ☐

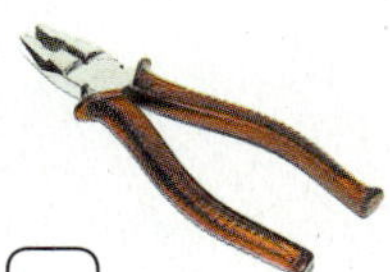

i. ☐

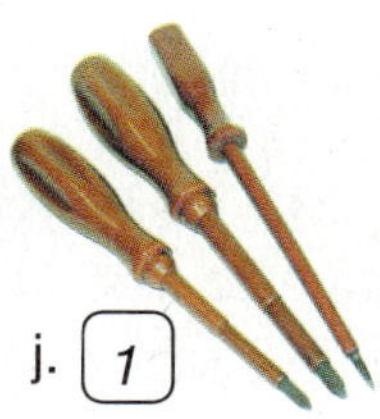

j. [1]

B List the above tools under the following headings.

power tools: ______________________

machine tools: ______________________

hand tools: *vice* ______________________

____

involve, v – beinhalten
manufacture – Fertigung
assembly – Montage
trainee – Auszubildende/r
mechanical engineering – Maschinenbau
power tool – Elektrowerkzeug
machine tool – Werkzeugmaschine
(combination) pliers – (Kombi-)zange
spanner – Schraubenschlüssel
square – Winkel
column drill – Ständerbohrmaschine
vice / bench vice – Bankschraubstock
hacksaw – Bügelsäge
angle grinder – Winkelschleifer
adjustable wrench – Rollgabelschlüssel

1 Visiting a workshop

Christian is an *apprentice* in his first year of training at CarFit, a car *manufacturer*. He has got a visitor from the States, Sarah, who is taking part in a trainee *exchange* project. After welcoming Sarah in the *reception* hall of his company, he shows her around the general workshop, which is on the *shop floor*.

A Listen to the dialogue.
Name three tools Christian is talking about.

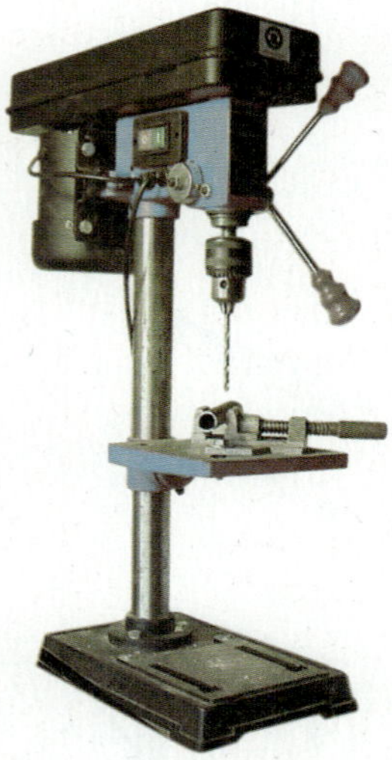

Christian: This is our general workshop, where we're trained in some basics of mechanical engineering.

Sarah: I see. What's that on top of those tables in the centre of this room?

Christian: Those tables are *octagonal workbenches* with bench vices on top.

Sarah: What are those vices used for?

Christian: They are used to *clamp* material, like a piece of metal. And then you can cut it with a hacksaw.

Sarah: OK, and the machine over there, between the windows?

Christian: That's a column drill, a machine tool that's really necessary in a general workshop, because you often have to *drill holes* into some metal.

Sarah: Oh, I see. Is it *complicated* to use?

Christian: No, not really. You see the machine table right in front of the column with the machine vice on top. It moves up and down the *vertical slide*. Clamp the *drill* into the *drill chuck*.
The machine table is lifted up the vertical slide near the drill *tip*.

Sarah: OK, and now we are ready to drill?

Christian: Right. But don't forget to put on some *goggles* as eye *protection* before you start drilling. And, Sarah, with long hair, you would also need a hairnet!

B Read the text. Make a list of all the *equipment* Christian shows Sarah in the general workshop. Give the German meanings.

C Work in groups. Look again at the illustrated tools at the beginning of the Unit. Discuss which of them are used in a garage/service station. Present your results to the class.

D Work in groups. Think of any tools used in a garage that are **not** illustrated. Use a dictionary if necessary.

apprentice – Lehrling
manufacturer – Hersteller
exchange – Austausch
reception – Empfang
shop floor – Werkstattetage
octagonal – achteckig
workbench – Werkbank
clamp, v – (ein)spannen
drill – bohren; Bohrer
hole – Loch
complicated – kompliziert
vertical slide – Senkrechtschlitten
drill chuck – Bohrfutter
tip – Spitze
goggles – Schutzbrille
protection – Schutz
equipment – Ausstattung

2 Working with tools

A Read the text. What kind of drill are they using? ______________________

Christian and Sarah have to do a practical exercise. They have to cut a metal *plate* to 400 mm *length* and 60 mm *width*. After that they have to work the metal plate to the length of a tenth of a mm and with four *right angles*. This must be done with a *roughing file* and a *finishing file*. The right angles are checked with a square, and the *edges* are *deburred* with a file. When this job is finished they have to *mark* four holes with a *diameter* of 5 mm in the corners of the metal plate. The marking is done with a *scriber*. Then they *centre punch* the marks and are ready for drilling with a *twist* drill. After drilling they *countersink* the hole.

B Work in pairs and match the sentences.

How do you hold the metal plate for cutting?

Clamp it in the bench vice.

1. ☐ How do you shorten the metal plate?
2. ☐ Which machine do you use for drilling the holes?
3. ☐ How do you find out if the edges are at a right angle?
4. ☐ How do you file the metal plate to be exact?
5. ☐ What do you do with the scriber?
6. ☐ How do you centre the marks for the holes?

a. Mark the holes you are going to drill.
b. Check them with a square.
c. Use a centre punch and a hammer.
d. Cut it with a hacksaw.
e. First rough the surface with a roughing file, then finish it with a finishing file.
f. Use the column drill.

plate – Platte
length – Länge
width – Breite
right angle – rechter Winkel
roughing file – Schruppfeile
finishing file – Schlichtfeile
edge – Kante
debur, v – entgraten
mark, v – anreißen
diameter – Durchmesser
scriber – Anreißnadel
centre punch, v – körnen; Körner
twist drill – Spiralbohrer
countersink, v – kegelsenken

3 Bench work

A Listen to the following dialogue about preparing the work place for bench work. Note down the main points. The words in the word box below will help you.

B Listen again. Then give a short summary in German.

4 Spot on grammar

The imperative (Die Befehlsform)

Der Befehlssatz beginnt mit dem Verb (Zeitwort), das im Infinitiv (Grundform) ohne **to** verwendet wird.

to work: ***Work*** *at the bench plate.*
to read: ***Read*** *the instructions.*
to forget: ***Don't forget*** *your pliers.*

- Work in pairs. Find ten different imperatives in Unit 1.

______________________ ______________________

______________________ ______________________

______________________ ______________________

______________________ ______________________

5 Spot on safety

- Look at the *safety* signs below and match them with the phrases that give the meanings.

1. 2. 3. 4. 5. 6.

a. ☐ Follow the emergency exit sign!

b. ☐ Don't smoke!

c. ☐ Don't walk here!

d. ☐ Warning! *Toxic* material!

e. ☐ Don't work with open fire!

f. ☐ Warning! High *voltage*!

section steel – U-Stahl
drawer – Schublade
measure, v – messen
guard plate – Schutzblech
vice jaw – Schraubstockbacken
scratch, v – (ver)kratzen
surface – Oberfläche
rag – Lappen
instructor – Werkstattlehrer; Meister
safety – Sicherheit
toxic – giftig
voltage – Spannung

UNIT 2

The car factory

Here are some of the main *departments* in a modern automobile *manufacturing facility*.

1. Press Shop
2. Body Shop
3. Paint Shop
4. Final Assembly
5. Logistics
6. Shipping

A Match the departments to the photos on the right.

B Now match the departments to the work done in them.

a. ☐ *installing* parts into the car
b. ☐ *supplying* the parts to the production lines
c. 1 *stamping* parts
d. ☐ *treating* the surface
e. ☐ *in charge* of sending the products to the *dealers*
f. ☐ *welding* parts together

department – Abteilung
manufacture, v – fertigen; herstellen
facility – Einrichtung
Press Shop – Presswerk
Body Shop – Produktion, Fertigung
Paint Shop – Lackiererei
Final Assembly – Endmontage
Logistics – Logistik
Shipping – Versand
install, v – einbauen
supply, v – liefern; versorgen
stamp, v – pressen
treat, v – behandeln
in charge – verantwortlich
dealer – Händler
weld, v – schweißen

1 A factory visit

Christian, the apprentice mechanic at CarFit, is telling Sarah and Mike, another exchange apprentice from England, about the factory visit planned for next week.

A Listen to the dialogue and read the text at the same time.

Christian: Hi Mike. Hi Sarah. How're things?
Sarah: Well, just great, really. Mike's got a problem, though.
Christian: Oh! What's wrong, Mike?
Mike: I was ironing a shirt yesterday evening and I dropped the iron on my toe. Pity I wasn't wearing my safety shoes at the time. Anyway, the pain has almost gone now.
Christian: Well, I hope it won't stop you from coming on our factory tour next week.
Sarah: I haven't heard anything about a *plant* tour. When's it on?
Christian: Monday afternoon. Our instructor is going to take us around the factory for two hours.
Mike: Sounds great. What's he going to show us?
Christian: The whole facility, I hope … from start to finish.
Sarah: Come on, Christian. Tell us a bit more, will you? Where're we going to start?

B Now listen to the rest of the dialogue. Which three main areas of the factory are they going to visit? The words in the box on the next page will help you.

1. ______________________
2. ______________________
3. ______________________

C Listen to the dialogue again.

They aren't going to visit one special area. What is it called? ______________________

Why can't they go there next week? ______________________

____

D Listen to the dialogue for details. Pay special attention to the technical vocabulary. Sort the following words into the four manufacturing areas *mentioned* in the dialogue.

welding gun	electrical *wiring*
robot	*marriage*
sparks	*die*
side panel	*body part*
dip	*immersion bath*
chassis	

E Look at the *tapescript* at the back of the book. Read it to yourself and underline any vocabulary you do not understand.

F Get into groups of three. Help each other with an explanation or a translation of the words in the transcript you do not know. Read the dialogue aloud, each person reading one role. Exchange roles. Read it again.

G Close your books. Write down as many technical words and phrases as you can remember from the dialogue. Give the sheet of paper to a classmate and ask him/her to translate the words for you.

plant – Fabrik
sheet metal – Stahlblech; Pressteil
body part – Karosserieteil
die (press) – Stempel, Presswerkzeug
weigh, v – wiegen
side panel – Seitenblech
spark – Funke
welding gun – Schweißpistole
dip, v – (ein)tauchen
immersion bath – Tauchbad
restricted area – Sperrzone
protective clothes – Schutzkleidung
wiring – Leitungen
marriage – Hochzeit
chassis – Chassis, Fahrgestell
mention, v – erwähnen
responsibility – Verantwortlichkeit
consist of, v – bestehen aus
responsible – verantwortlich

2 Plant structure

A Read the following phrases used to describe plant structure and *responsibilities*.

Plant Manager
Body Shop
Main Underbody
Robot maintenance specialist

"It's the boss's idea – Benson's the best worker in the office."

1. The car plant is **divided into** various departments.
2. Each department is **split up into** teams.
3. Each team *consists of* a number of specialists.
4. The Press Shop is *responsible* **for** manufacturing body parts.
5. Shipping is **in charge of** sending the products to the dealers.

B Write similar sentences about your own company. Ask your teacher for help, if necessary.

________________ divided into ________________

________________ split up into ________________

________________ consists of ________________

________________ responsible for ________________

________________ in charge of ________________

3 Spot on grammar

Going to-future *(going to-Zukunft)*
Going to wird verwendet, um (persönliche) Planungen und Vorhaben auszudrücken.

When are you ***going to build*** *the new training centre?*
We are ***going to build*** *the new training centre next year.*
We are ***not going to knock down*** *the old one.*

• Work in pairs. A co-worker is going to Sunderland, England, for a week to visit a service station (or a workshop). Discuss the plans for the trip.

Student A
Prepare to ask your co-worker as many questions as possible using the going to-future. Use the question forms and the verbs in the boxes on the right.

When are you going to go?

Where ...?	go
When ...?	stay
What ...?	do
Why ...?	work
Who ...?	spend
How ...?	meet
How much ...?	see
How many ...?	come
How long ...?	cost

Student B
Answer the questions as realistically as possible.
Use complete sentences. Think about the following:

I'm going to go in May.

place – hotel – cost – travel – people – job – time – free time

4 Spot on safety

A What kinds of protective *clothing* were mentioned in the dialogues in this Unit? ______________________

B Match the following protective *gear* with the illustrations.

☐ ear protectors
☐ safety shoes
☐ safety glasses
☐ safety helmet
☐ rigger's gloves
☐ boilersuit
☐ cup mask

1. 
2. 
3. 
4. 
5. 
6. 
7. 

clothing – Kleidung
gear – Ausrüstung
rigger's gloves – Arbeitshandschuhe
boilersuit – Overall

UNIT 3

Vehicles

Over the last 20 years car manufacturers have designed many new types of cars to *meet the demands* of the market. These are often called *niche* cars. Some of these have become so popular that they now *outsell* many *common* types. An example of this is the *sport utility vehicle* or *SUV* as it is often called. Another modern manufacturing strategy is to use one platform as a basis for different models and even different *brands*.

A Think of some cars that are built on the same platform.

B Match the types of vehicles with the photos below.

1. *saloon/sedan*
2. cabriolet/convertible
3. sport utility vehicle (SUV)
4. coupé
5. *estate car/station wagon*
6. *multi-purpose* vehicle
7. *limousine*

1

meet demands – Anforderungen erfüllen
niche – Nische
outsell, v – mehr als … verkaufen
common – alltäglich
sport utility vehicle (SUV) – Geländewagen
brand – Marke
saloon/sedan – Limousine
estate car/station wagon – Kombiwagen
multi-purpose – Mehrzweck-
limousine – Luxuslimousine

C Work in pairs and discuss. What kind of vehicles are missing from the list above?

1 The Body Shop

Steffen Berger is a *production fitter* in the Body Shop where the *body shell* is produced. He is responsible for *maintaining* the manufacturing equipment and making sure that the machines don't break down. He is presenting his area and day-to-day job to Sarah and Mike.

A Read the following text. What are Steffen Berger's responsibilities?

I usually get to the factory at about 5.30 in the morning when I'm on the morning *shift*. We operate a three shift system. I never have to work nights because we have a permanent night shift. I mostly *clock in* just before six after changing into my boilersuit in the *locker-room*.

The first thing I do is check if there've been any *major* breakdowns on the line during the night shift. We discuss what we have to do and then we carry out *maintenance* on the *faulty* parts. We repair some parts and *replace* others. I usually work on the main *underbody sub-assembly* line. The machines and *conveyors* are fully automated.
Handling robots take the *metal panels, brackets* and *members* and place them on a *jig pallet* which moves along on top of the conveyor. They are *tack-welded* in the *framing station* to hold the parts together. The jig pallet moves on to the *spot welding* station where robots join the parts with their welding guns. They also do *stud welding* and *rivet welding*.
The main sub-assemblies are the underbody, the *engine compartment*, the side-walls, the doors and the roof. When they are all welded, we check the body shell for *smoothness* and *grind* the *rough* areas if necessary.
I don't normally spend the whole day working on the machines. I often meet with the engineers to see how the quality can be *improved*.

B True or false? Give reasons for your answers.

	true	false	
1.	☐	☐	They grind all the body shell to make it smoother.
2.	☐	☐	The parts are put onto a jig pallet which is on a conveyor.
3.	☐	☐	Steffen Berger is an assembly line worker.
4.	☐	☐	He makes sure the machines break down.
5.	☐	☐	He normally works on the underbody line.
6.	☐	☐	He works two shifts.
7.	☐	☐	He starts work at 5.30.

production fitter – Fertigungsmechaniker/in
body shell – Rohbaukarrosse
maintain, v – instandhalten
shift – Schicht
clock in, v – (Zeituhr) stempeln
locker-room – Umkleideraum
major – größer
maintenance – Instandhaltung

C Write a suitable verb from the box in front of each phrase below. Use each verb only once. Be careful, there may be more than one possibility.

present	discuss	check	spend
improve	operate	carry out	make sure

1. *present* your responsibilities
2. ______ the machines don't break down
3. ______ a framing station
4. ______ for smoothness
5. ______ maintenance
6. ______ what to do
7. ______ the whole day
8. ______ vehicle quality

faulty – fehlerhaft, schadhaft
replace, v – ersetzen
underbody – Unterboden
sub-assembly – Baugruppe
handling robot – Laderoboter
metal panel – Beplankung
bracket – Stütze
member – Träger
jig pallet – Bauteilträger
conveyor – Förderer
tack-weld, v – heftschweißen
framing station – Aufbaustation
spot welding – Punktschweißen
stud welding – Bolzenschweißen
rivet welding – Nietschweißen
engine compartment – Motorraum
smoothness – Ebenheit
grind, v – schleifen
rough – rau
improve, v – verbessern

2 Spot on grammar

The simple present tense (Gegenwart)

Das **simple present** wird verwendet
- bei regelmäßigen Handlungen mit **usually, normally, always, never, sometimes, often**
- bei Gewohnheiten
- bei allgemein bekannten Tatsachen und Aussagen

*I **usually clock in** at 6 a.m.*
*I **don't normally work** on Saturdays.*
*What kind of car **do you drive**?*

• Work in pairs. Look at the answers that Steffen Berger gave to some questions. What were the questions? Look at the text in **1A** if you are stuck.

1. ______? In the Body Shop.
2. ______? For maintaining the equipment.
3. ______? At about 5.30 in the morning.
4. ______? What we have to do during the shift.
5. *How do the metal panels get onto the jig pallet*? The handling robots do that.
6. ______? With their welding guns.
7. ______? Because it isn't smooth enough.

8. ____? No, not the whole day.

9. ______________________________________? With the engineers.

10. ____________________________________? To discuss how quality can be improved.

3 A class survey

A Work in small groups. Think up five questions in total about the habits and routines of your classmates. Choose your questions carefully.
Limit your questions to work, *vocational school*, or cars.

What do you want to be?

I want to be a mechanic/a fitter/an electrician/…

How do you get to work every day?

… by car/by bus/by train/…

B Split up and interview all your classmates including those in your own group. Note down their answers. Then make a report to the class on your findings.

Most of the people here (ride a scooter).
Three out of five (want to be a mechanic).
80 % (per cent) of the …/Some of the …
Very few people …/None of the …

4 Spot on safety

● Mike has just seen the notice below in the washroom. He wants to know what it means. Tell him in English in your own words. Make sure you get all the important points. Use a dictionary if necessary.

Stolper- oder Rutschgefahr besteht bei
- **herumliegenden Kabeln und Leitungen**
- **Türschwellen**
- **Unebenheiten im Boden**
- **eingeschränkter Sicht durch das Tragen von Gegenständen**
- **verschütteten Ölen und Fetten**
- **schlechtem Schuhwerk**
- **nassen, vereisten, verdreckten Wegen, Böden, Leitern, Treppen**

Give Mike some good advice about what to do.

You should/shouldn't …

vocational school – Berufsschule

UNIT 4

Process planning and processes

Before *joining* and *assembling*, it is important to plan the material of the parts to be joined such as *steel* and aluminium or *plastics*. Then you think about the different joining methods, *e.g. screwing*, welding or *bonding*, because each joining method *requires* different tools. For screwing, screwdrivers and spanners or wrenches are used to *tighten* or *loosen screws*, *bolts* and *nuts*. For gas welding, a *welding torch* is needed as well as gas and *oxygen* cylinders. If you have to bond plastics and steel, for example, you will need a *suitable adhesive*.

- Which car parts in the picture above are screwed or welded? Which parts would be bonded? Name the necessary tools from the text.

The rear light is screwed with a screwdriver.

underbody – *headlight* – engine compartment – *rear* door – rear seat

join, v – fügen, verbinden
assemble, v – zusammenbauen
steel – Stahl
plastics – Plastik
e.g. = for example – z. B. (zum Beispiel)
screw, v – schrauben
bond, v – kleben
require, v – erfordern
tighten, v – (fest) anziehen
loosen, v – lösen
screw – Schraube
bolt – Bolzen, Schraube
nut – Mutter
welding torch – Schweißbrenner
oxygen – Sauerstoff
suitable – passend
adhesive – Klebstoff
headlight – Scheinwerfer
rear – hintere, Rück-

1 Process planning

A Listen to the dialogue. When are the bolts of the *pipe bracket knocked off*?

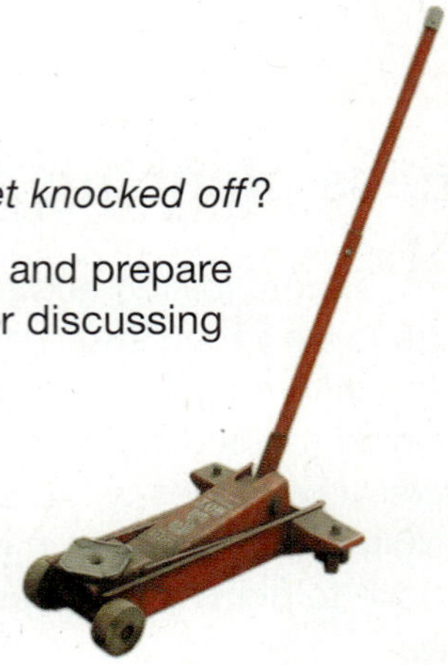

Sarah, Mike and Christian have been instructed by Herr Berger to plan and prepare the process of exchanging an *exhaust* system. They are sitting together discussing what they have to do.

Christian: All right. What are we going to do first?
Mike: … and which tools will be needed?
Sarah: Hold on a minute. I think we've got to find out first if the *car lift* is *available*, because if not, we've got to use a *jack*.
Christian: You're right. And of course, one of us has to get the new exhaust.
Mike: OK. I can do that; I have to go to the *Spare Parts Store* anyway.
Sarah: Fine, and don't forget to write down the correct part number before you go.
Christian: OK. Now, what about the tools? I think a spanner and an adjustable wrench are necessary.
Mike: Yes, but what happens if the bolts of the old pipe bracket are *rusty* and can't be loosened at all?
Sarah: Well, in that case a hammer and a *cold chisel* will help.

Mike: Yes, that's true. The bolts are just knocked off.
Christian: And we might have the same problem with the exhaust *pipe*.
Sarah: So, the pipe has to be cut with either a hacksaw or an angle grinder.
Mike: Right. And the pipe of the new exhaust probably has to be welded, which means we'll need some welding equipment.
Christian: I don't think so. Normally, the diameter of the exhaust pipe is big enough at the end and it's *adjustable* as well … so it can be *mounted* with a new pipe bracket.
Sarah: Fine. Looks like everything is settled now, so let's get started.

B Read the text again. Take the roles of Sarah, Mike and Christian. Make a dialogue discussing the process plan of exchanging an exhaust system. The phrases below will help you. But be careful: they are not in the right order. Then present your dialogue to the class.

Christian:

First we have to plan the job.
All right. So let's drive the car onto the car lift.
Yes, so we can knock off the bolts if they are rusty and can't be unscrewed.
The exhaust must have the correct part number.

pipe bracket – Rohrschelle
knock off, v – (etwas) abschlagen
exhaust – Auspuff
car lift – Hebebühne
be available – zur Verfügung stehen
jack – Wagenheber
Spare Parts Store – Ersatzteillager
rusty – rostig, verrostet
cold chisel – Flachmeißel
pipe – Rohr
adjustable – verstellbar
mount, v – montieren
spare part – Ersatzteil

Sarah:

That means the work place and the material must be prepared …
So the number has to be written down. Then you have to get the exhaust from the Spare Parts Store.
And a hacksaw or an angle grinder will be needed in case the old pipe is also rusty.
That's easy, because it's just done with a screwdriver.

Mike:

… and the necessary tools.
Do we have a cold chisel and a hammer?
In that case we'll also need a new pipe bracket to mount the exhaust pipe.

2 A dented wing

Your task is to exchange a *dented* front *wing*, so the *wing apron* and the headlight have to be *demounted* as well.

A Work in groups. Plan the process by putting the phrases below into the right order.

- [1] Prepare the necessary tools.
- [ ] *Dispose of* the old wing in the *scrap* container.
- [ ] *Unscrew* the bolts of the front wing and put them on the *tray*.
- [ ] Take off the dented front wing.
- [ ] Loosen the bolts of the wing apron and put them on the tray.
- [ ] Unscrew the screws and bolts of the headlight.
- [ ] Mount the new front wing.
- [ ] Put the used screws and bolts on a tray.
- [ ] Take off the headlight carefully and put it on the tray.
- [ ] Take off the wing apron.

B Work in pairs. Match the tools in the illustrations below with the operation steps above. Be careful, you don't need tools for **all** the operation steps.

dented – verbeult
wing – Kotflügel
wing apron – Motorraumseitenteil
demount, v – abbauen, abmontieren
dispose, v, of – entsorgen
scrap – Schrott
unscrew, v – abschrauben
tray – Tablett

3 Spot on grammar

Simple present: The passive voice (Das Passiv in der einfachen Gegenwart)

Im technischen Englisch wird das Passiv sehr häufig verwendet, um das Wesentliche einer Handlung hervorzuheben. Das Passiv wird gebildet mit einer Form von **be** und der **3. Verbform** des Vollverbs.

The process plan ***is made*** *before the job* ***is started.***

wrench – Schraubenschlüssel
torque wrench – Drehmomentschlüssel
plaster – Pflaster
first aid kit – Erste-Hilfe-Ausrüstung, Verbandszeug
run out of, v – kein … mehr haben

• Write complete sentences in the passive with the help of the words and phrases below.

car lift – with the start and stop button – start

The car lift ***is started*** *with the start and stop button.*

1. wheel nuts – with a nut *wrench* – loosen

2. work place – before – starting to operate – prepare

3. wheel nuts – with a *torque wrench* – tighten

4. rusty bolt – with a cold chisel – knock off

5. old wing – in the scrap container – dispose of

6. spare parts – by the correct part number – check

7. rusty pipe – with an angle grinder – cut off

8. after finishing the work – work place – clean

4 Spot on safety

• Listen to the following telephone dialogue. Write down who is speaking, what has happened, why it has happened, and what first aid steps are planned.

UNIT 5

The body shell and body repair

A Fill in the missing numbers for parts of the body shell. Use the word box for help.

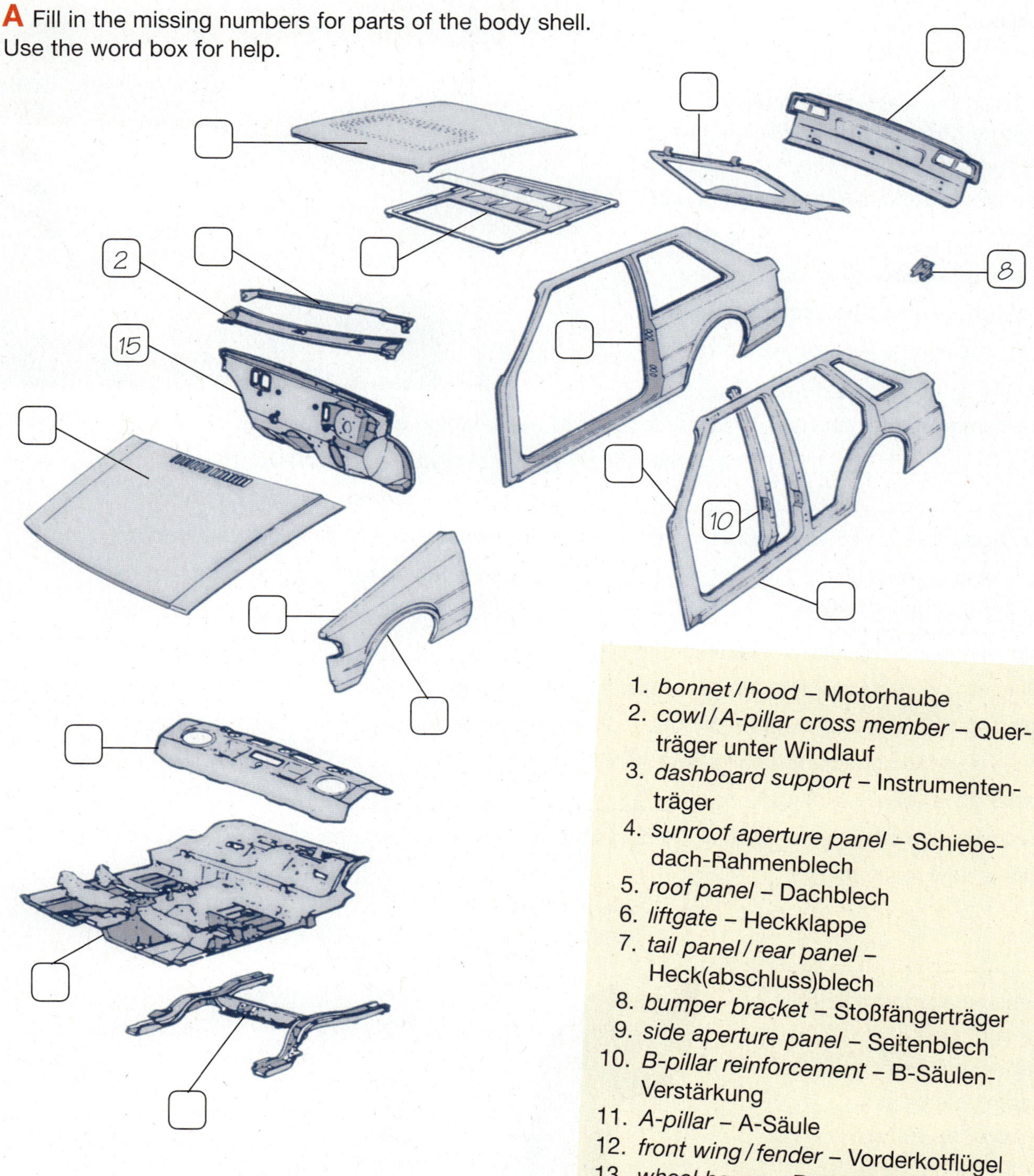

1. *bonnet / hood* – Motorhaube
2. *cowl / A-pillar cross member* – Querträger unter Windlauf
3. *dashboard support* – Instrumententräger
4. *sunroof aperture panel* – Schiebedach-Rahmenblech
5. *roof panel* – Dachblech
6. *liftgate* – Heckklappe
7. *tail panel / rear panel* – Heck(abschluss)blech
8. *bumper bracket* – Stoßfängerträger
9. *side aperture panel* – Seitenblech
10. *B-pillar reinforcement* – B-Säulen-Verstärkung
11. *A-pillar* – A-Säule
12. *front wing / fender* – Vorderkotflügel
13. *wheel house* – Radlauf
14. *door sill* – Türschweller
15. *firewall* – Spritzwand
16. *cross member* – Querträger
17. *underbody* – Unterboden
18. *rear shelf panel* – Heckablageblech

B Work in pairs. Write down more parts of the body shell in German. Translate them, with the help of a dictionary if necessary.

1 Dent repair

Steffen Berger is explaining the basics of dent repair to the exchange trainees.

A Read the text and fill in the missing phrases from the box below.

The first job is to pull the dent out until the ① ____________________ is as close as possible to its original *shape*. Bring the *level* of the dent up to about 3 mm below the level of the surrounding metal. ② ____________________ the dent from the rear using a *soft-face hammer*. While doing this hold a block of wood ③ ____________________ the opposite side of the metal to *absorb* the *blows*. This also ④ ____________________________________ *stretching*. Now *remove* the paint from the *damaged* area and the surrounding metal. You do this with a *wire brush*, some sandpaper or a *sanding drill*. ⑤ ____________________ with a screwdriver to *provide* a good *grip* for the *filler*. Now it's time to ⑥ ______________________ to the prepared area. Bit by bit *add* thin *layers* until the level is just above the ⑦ ______________________. *Sand* the hardened filler with *progressively* finer *grades* of sandpaper, starting with 180-*grit* sandpaper and finishing with a 600-grit wet-or-dry paper. *Wrap* the sandpaper around a wooden block to make sure the surface of the filler will be ⑧ ____________________. *Rinse* the wet-or-dry paper *occasionally* with water to ⑨ ____________________________. Then rinse the repair area well with clean water until all the *dust* from the sanding operation is gone. The repaired area is now ready for ⑩ _________________ *primer*.

ensure a *smooth* finish
a light *coat* of
apply the filler paste
completely flat
score the surface
damaged area
firmly against
gently hammer out
surrounding metal
prevents the metal from

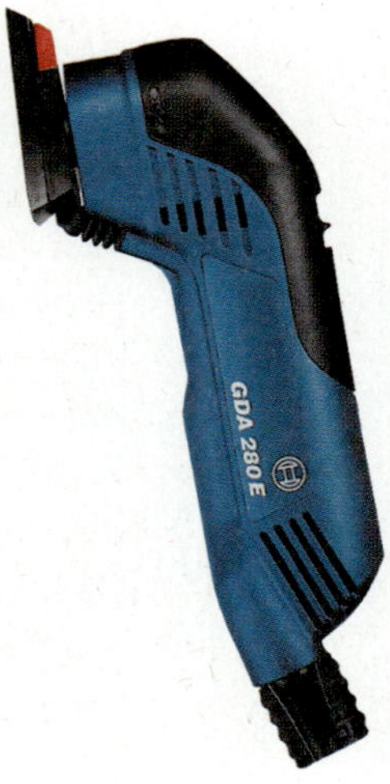

dent – Beule
shape – Form
level – Ebene, Niveau
soft-face hammer – Aluhammer
absorb, v – aufnehmen
blow – Schlag
stretch, v – ausdehnen
remove, v – entfernen
damaged – beschädigt
wire brush – Stahlbürste
sanding drill – Elektroschleifer
provide, v – sorgen für; versorgen
grip – Haftung
filler – Spachtelmasse
add, v – hinzufügen

B Listen to the completed text in **A** and check your answers.

C Write four different answers to the following questions. Make answers with **in order to**. What are the uses for blocks of wood in the body repair process? Why is rinsing used?

D Work by yourself. If you can't get at the dent from behind it is necessary to use a different technique to *straighten out* the metal. Use the following words to describe the process.

drill	*self-tapping screws*
small holes	*locking pliers*
deepest section	grip
damaged area	pull out
screw	

layer – Schicht
sand, v – schleifen
progressively – stufenweise
grade – Sorte, Grad
grit – Korn
wrap, v – einwickeln
rinse, v – spülen
occasionally – gelegentlich
dust – Staub
primer – Grundierung
smooth – glatt
coat – Schicht
apply, v – auftragen
score, v – kratzen
firmly – fest
gently – vorsichtig
prevent, v – verhindern
straighten out, v – ausbeulen
self-tapping screw – Blechschraube
locking pliers – Gripzange

E Look at the photo of the damaged vehicle. Which repair process is more suitable, **A** or **D**? Give reasons.

F Work in pairs. In German, write down the instructions for preparing and spray painting the damaged area (about 5 lines). Give the instructions to another pair to translate. Check them in groups of four. Present your best translations to the class.

2 Words and meanings

• Work in pairs. Look at the following sentences with a form of **apply** in them. Find out the different meanings. What does **apply** mean in German in each case?

1. The robot applies three layers of paint to the body shell. ____________________
2. Apply the *brake* gently to slow the car down. ____________________
3. I applied for a job at the factory and was *accepted*. ____________________
4. That rule does not apply to us. We can do what we want. ____________________

brake – Bremse
accept, v – annehmen

3 Spot on grammar

Adverbs (Umstandswörter)

Das Adverb (Umstandswort) dient zur näheren Beschreibung eines Verbs (Zeitwortes) oder eines Adjektivs (Eigenschaftswortes).

*He drove too **fast**.*
*It is **absolutely** perfect.*
*It works **beautifully**.*

- Look at the text in **1A** again. Underline and name all the examples of the use of adverbs in the text. List them. How many different adverbs were you able to find?

4 Writing a fax

- Write a fax. You are working at a car repair shop. A customer has brought in her car to be repaired. There is a small dent in the front wing. After examining the car you have to write a short fax to the customer telling her what has to be done, the time needed, the cost and when she can pick up her car (about 50 words).

FAX

From: *CarFit Service and Repair Ltd, Siemens Str. 14-16, 70173 Stuttgart*
Tel.: +49(0)711 5461540, Fax: +49(0)711 54615412

To: *Ms Martha Roberts, Im Holderbusch 5, 70372 Bad Cannstatt*

Date: *19 May 2003*

Dear Ms Roberts,

5 Spot on safety

- What protective gear do you need in a body repair shop? Make a list and compare it with a classmate's list.

UNIT 6

Automotive electrics

A modern automobile has a lot of electronic equipment and electric motors: a stereo set with a CD player, a *central locking* system, *power windows* and *ABS* are standard equipment. It is said that a limousine is *equipped* with as many electric motors as the Space Shuttle. That is why an automotive electrician needs a standard set of hand tools *to deal with* all the electrics in a car.

a. Abisolierzange ☐ 2

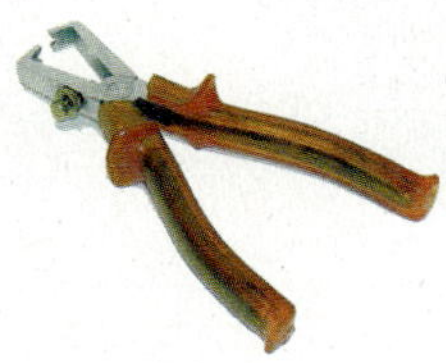

b. Flachrundzange ☐

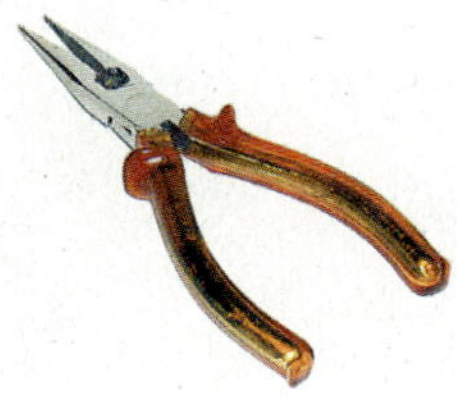

c. Seitenschneider mit Handschutz ☐

d. Schraubendreher (Schlitz-/Kreuzschlitz-) ☐

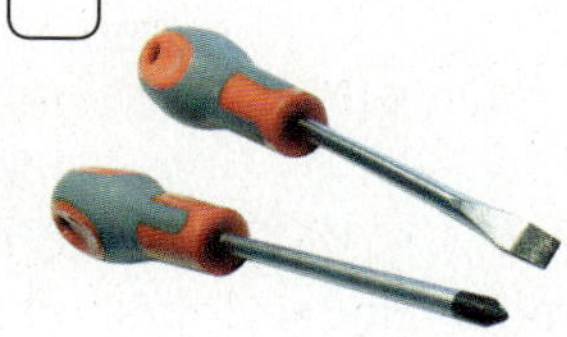

e. Kneifzange ☐ 6

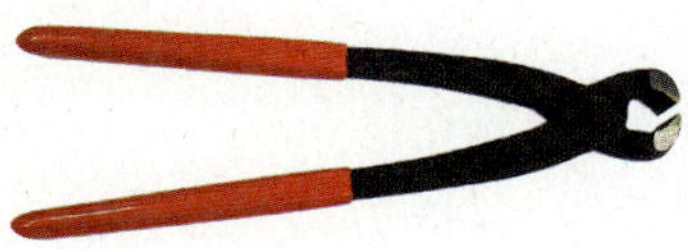

f. Multimeter ☐

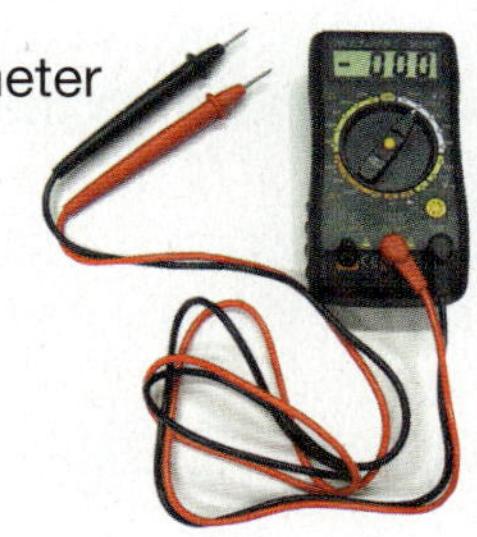

g. Phasenprüfer ☐

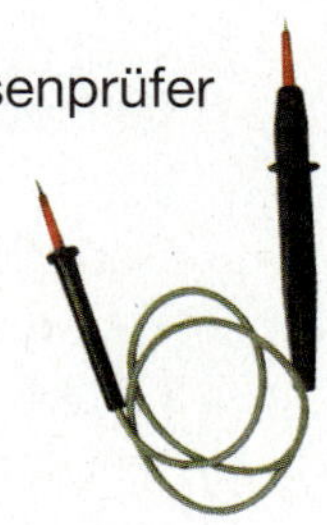

A The English names of an electrician's hand tools are in the box on the right. Match them with the illustrations above.

1. cutting nippers with hand guard
2. wire stripper/wire stripping pliers
3. screwdrivers (slotted and cross head)
4. round nose pliers
5. multimeter
6. pincers
7. mains tester

B What are the tools used for? The verbs in the box will help you.

pull out – check (2x) – cut – strip – tighten or loosen – *nip off*

Mains testers are used to check a live wire.

automotive electrics – Kfz-Elektrik
central locking – Zentralverriegelung
power windows – elektrische Fensterheber
ABS = anti-lock braking system – Antiblockiersystem
be equipped – ausgestattet sein
deal with – sich befassen mit
nip off, v – abzwicken

1 Basic automotive electrics

Today Christian, Sarah and Mike are learning something about *basic* automotive electrics. Steffen Berger, their instructor, explains some of the most common electric equipment that CarFit builds into their cars.

A Listen to the dialogue. What are the two functions of a *generator*?

Steffen Berger: First of all there's the 12 volt car battery.

Mike: Yes, I know, it supplies all the electric equipment with the necessary *current*.

Steffen Berger: *Compare* it with the *mains* in a building.

Sarah: Oh, that's easy. In a building we have ***alternating** current*, and the 12 volt battery provides the car with ***direct** current*.

Christian: Yes, that's right, and it starts the car with the *starter motor*.

Steffen Berger: Well, looks like you already know a lot. But the battery isn't powerful enough to supply all the electric equipment. So it gets help from the generator.

Mike: *That reminds me* of a trip to Spain last summer, you know, when a few friends and I were travelling through the night. Suddenly our car headlights began *losing* power.

Sarah: Sounds *exciting*. What did you do? Did you check the generator?

Mike: Yes, and we found that the *V-belt* was broken.

Christian: Could you do anything about it?

Mike: Yes, luckily we had a *spare* V-belt with us and the necessary tools to mount it.

Steffen Berger: Well done! So what do we learn from this about the functions of the generator?

Christian: Well, I guess it's absolutely necessary to supply **all** the electric equipment in a car with power …

Sarah: … and, of course, to *charge* the battery *permanently*.

B Work in groups. Think of some good reasons why the electrics listed in the box below are necessary. The phrases on the next page will help you. Present your results to the class.

generator
starter motor
battery
radiator
indicator
ignition
wiring harness

basic – grundlegend
generator – Lichtmaschine
current – elektrischer Strom
compare, v – vergleichen
mains (electricity supply) – Stromnetz
alternating current (AC) – Wechselstrom
direct current (DC) – Gleichstrom
starter motor – Starter
remind, v: That reminds me of … – erinnern: Das erinnert mich an …
lose, v – verlieren
exciting – aufregend, interessant
V-belt – Keilriemen
spare – Ersatz-
charge, v – (Batterie) aufladen
permanent(ly) – ständig, regelmäßig

It consists of all the wires in a car.

If the car doesn't have it, it can't run at all.

If this isn't working, the car won't start.

This is very important to supply the car electrics with power.

It is necessary to prevent the car engine from overheating.

It is the process of *generating* the sparks to *ignite* the *fuel*.

If it isn't used, other car drivers can't see which way you are going to turn.

radiator – Kühler
indicator – Blinker
ignition – Zündung
wiring harness – Kabelbaum
generate, v – erzeugen
ignite, v – zünden
fuel – Kraftstoff

wiring harness – It consists of all the wires in a car.

C A spare parts dealer from Cork, Ireland, phones CarFit and is *put through* to the Spare Parts Store. Sarah, who is working there for a week, answers the phone.

Listen to the telephone *enquiry* and note down all the important facts in German.

D Write a *memo* for Steffen Berger in German. The memo should have all the important information, *i.e.* names, addresses, reason for the enquiry, part number.

2 Spot on grammar

First conditional clauses (if-Sätze)

Im **if**-Satz steht das Verb in der Gegenwart **(present tense)**, im Hauptsatz steht das Verb in der Zukunft **(will-future)**. Die Satzstellung im **if**-Satz ist die gleiche wie im Hauptsatz (S-P-O). Der **if**-Satz kann am Anfang stehen und wird durch Komma abgetrennt. Der **if**-Satz kann aber auch am Ende stehen. In diesem Fall wird kein Komma gesetzt.

If the battery ***is*** *empty, the starter motor* ***won't work****.*

The radio ***will stop*** *playing if the fuse* ***blows****.*

put through – (Telefon) verbinden
enquiry – Anfrage
message – Nachricht
urgent(ly) – dringend
appreciate, v – dankbar sein für
circuit diagram – Schaltplan
forward to, v – weiterleiten, -geben an
memo – Kurznachricht
i.e. (id est) – d. h. (das heißt)

• Ask your classmates to answer the following questions in complete sentences. The phrases in the box will help you.

1. What tool will you use if you *strip* an electric wire?
2. What will you have to use if you want to check the voltage of a car battery?
3. What will happen if the generator breaks down?
4. What will you have to do if the battery *conductors are corroded*?
5. What will the starter motor not do if the battery is empty?

have to clean
car battery / *go flat*
have to use / multimeter
use / wire stripper
starter motor / not work

3 Spot on safety

Many accidents happen as a result of contact with faulty equipment. That is why you must always follow certain safety rules.

• Put the words in the correct order.

electrical equipment / working / the / on / *mains* / before / switch off

Switch off the mains before working on electrical equipment.

1. any / cables / damaged / don't use

____

2. wet hands / with / don't / electrical equipment / touch

____

3. use / the old one / when / always / a new fuse / is damaged

____

4. an *insulated* mains tester / use / always / live wiring / checking / when

____

fuse – Sicherung
fuse: the fuse blows – die Sicherung brennt durch
strip, v – abisolieren
battery: the battery goes flat – die Batterie wird schwach
conductor – (Elektrizität) Leiter
be corroded – korrodiert sein
mains – Stromnetz-Hauptschalter
insulated – isoliert

UNIT 7

Engine and drive train

engine – Motor
drive train – Antriebsstrang, Kraftübertragung
compound word – zusammengesetztes Wort

A Work in groups of three or four. Combine the words from the lists below to make *compound words*. They are all parts of an engine. Their translations are in the green box. Check the results with your classmates or your teacher.

1. cam	shaft	9. exhaust	screw
2. connecting	head	10. piston	dipstick
3. fly	filter	11. spark	plug
4. cylinder	fan	12. valve	pan
5. air	pump	13. oil	manifold
6. ribbed	wheel	14. oil drain	ring
7. radiator	V-belt	15. starter	spring
8. injection	rod	16. oil	pinion gear

B Label the direct injection petrol engine below with the English compound words from **A**. Which parts do not belong to this engine or cannot be seen in the picture?

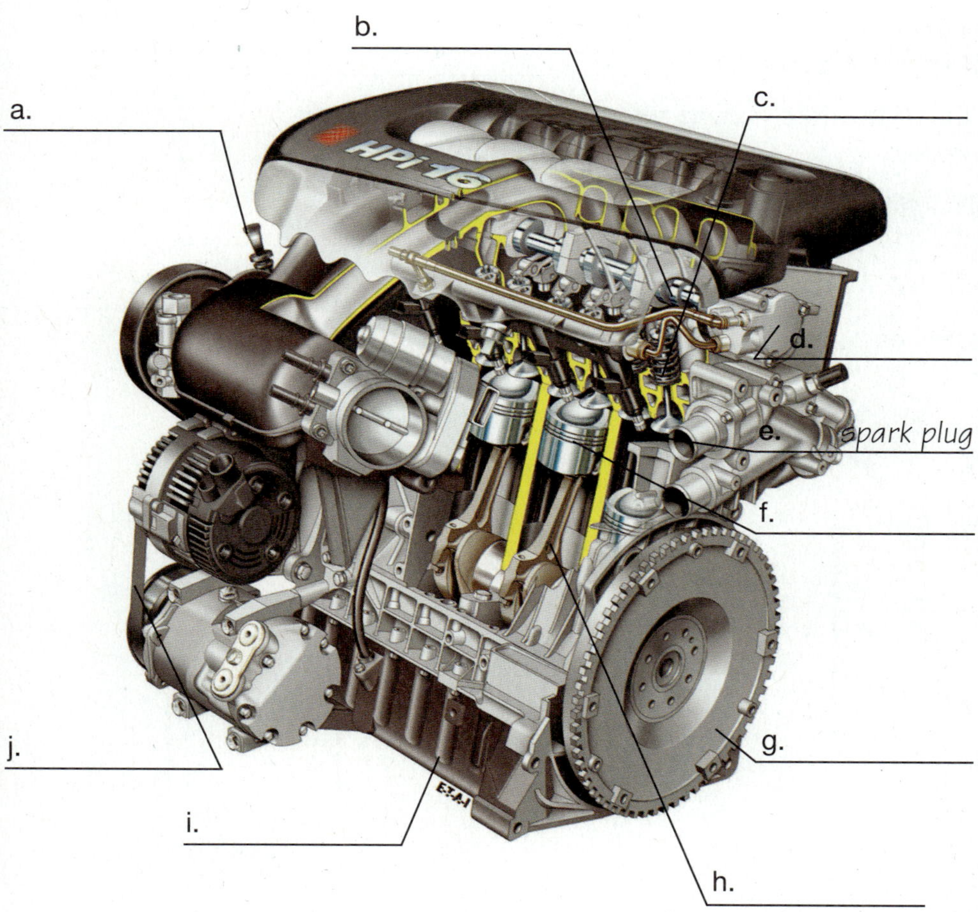

- ☐ Luftfilter
- ☐ Keilrippenriemen
- ☐ Nockenwelle
- ☐ Zündkerze
- ☐ Ölablassschraube
- ☐ Pleuel(-stange)
- ☐ Ventilfeder
- ☐ Anlasserritzel
- ☐ Auspuffkrümmer
- ☐ Zylinderkopf
- ☐ Kolbenring
- ☐ Ölmessstab
- ☐ Kühlerventilator
- ☐ Einspritzpumpe
- ☐ Ölwanne
- ☐ Schwungrad

1 The petrol engine

Steffen Berger is explaining the basics of engine technology to some international trainees.

In the *internal combustion engine* heat is *converted* into *motive power*. The engine works by burning a mixture of petrol and air in a cylinder containing a piston. The heat produced *causes* the air to *expand* and *force* down the piston, which turns a *crankshaft* connected to the wheels.

Most cars have a four-*stroke* engine. A stroke is a movement of the piston, either up to the top dead centre (TDC) or down to the bottom dead centre (BDC). In a four-stroke engine the engine repeats a *cycle* of actions in which the piston moves four times. These four strokes are called the **induction stroke**, the **compression stroke**, the **power stroke** and the **exhaust stroke**.

A What do TDC and BDC mean?

B Here is a description of the four strokes. Which is which?

1. The electric spark plug produces a spark and the petrol ignites, forcing the piston back down the cylinder.
2. The piston moves down and the *inlet valve* opens. The petrol and air mixture is *sucked* into the cylinder.
3. The *outlet valve* opens and the piston rises, forcing the exhaust gases out of the cylinder.
4. The inlet valve closes and the piston moves up, compressing the mixture.

C Label the pictures with the strokes.

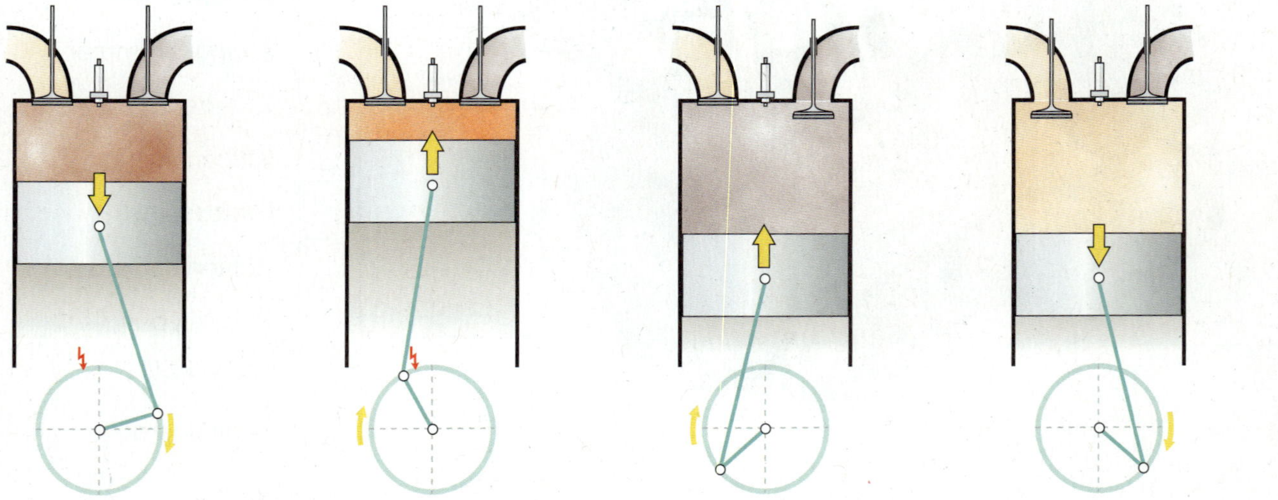

D In small groups write a short text explaining the differences between a petrol engine and a diesel engine.

Write about
- the grade of fuel
- the air *intake*
- when the fuel enters the cylinder
- the spark plug
- fuel ignition and compression.

internal combustion engine – Verbrennungsmotor
convert, v – umwandeln
motive power – Schub(-kraft)
cause, v – verursachen
expand, v – ausdehnen
force, v – drücken
crankshaft – Kurbelwelle
stroke – Takt, Hub
cycle – Kreislauf
induction stroke – Ansaugtakt
compression stroke – Verdichtungstakt
power stroke – Arbeitstakt
exhaust stroke – Ausstoßtakt
inlet (intake) valve – Einlassventil
suck, v – (an)saugen
outlet valve – Auslassventil

E Label the pictures with their English names.

____

____

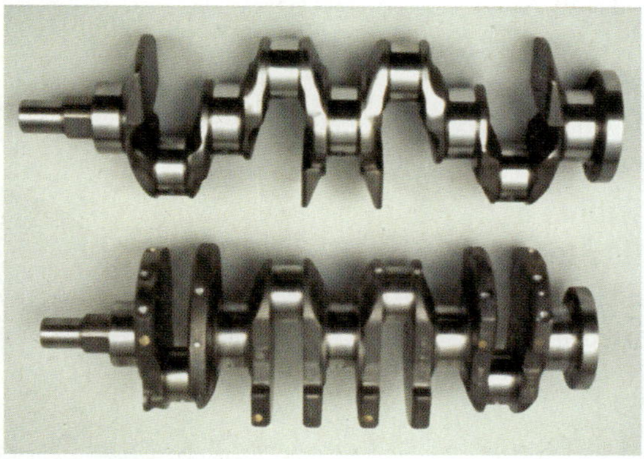

____

____

____

2 Fault analysis

A Find the right *cause* for each symptom.

Symptom	Cause
1. The engine *misfired*	oil *leaked* from the *gaskets*
2. Oil *consumption* was very high	the connecting rod *bearings* were worn
3. The engine *backfired*	a faulty spark plug
4. The engine lost power	an *intake manifold leak*
5. There were unusual noises from the engine	low cylinder compression

B Join the symptoms to the causes with **because** or **because of**.

*He crashed the car **because** he drove too fast.*

*He crashed the car **because of** (the) bad weather.*

cause – Ursache
leak, v – lecken, undicht sein
gasket – Dichtmanschette
misfire, v – zünden mit Zündaussetzern
consumption – Verbrauch
bearing – Lager
backfire, v – knallen (bei Fehlzündung)
intake manifold – Einlasskrümmer
leak – undichte Stelle

3 Spot on grammar

Simple past tense (Vergangenheit)
Das **simple past tense** wird verwendet bei Vorgängen, die in der Vergangenheit abgeschlossen wurden, meistens mit Zeitangabe. Signalwörter sind u.a.:
yesterday, in (1997), last year, 3 days ago, when ...

When ***did*** *the car* ***break down****? – It* ***broke down*** *yesterday morning.*
I ***didn't take*** *it to the service station in the afternoon.*

• Listen to the dialogue between Mike and Sarah. Write down the simple past tense verbs which you hear.

4 Do-it-Yourself

Christian's car was giving him trouble all last week. There were vibrations in the steering wheel and a *wobble* in the front wheels. On Friday afternoon he decided to look for the cause himself. Sarah and Mike came round to his garage to help him but when they arrived Christian had already demounted the front wheels.

A Read Christian's description of the process.

1. I applied the *hand brake* and blocked the rear wheels.
2. Then I loosened the bolts.
3. I *raised* the front of the vehicle and *supported* it.
4. I removed the bolts and demounted the front wheels.
5. I noticed something on the *wheel rim* and saw the damaged *drive shaft*.
6. Finally I decided it was too difficult to repair myself.

B Ask Christian about the process he described in **A**.

1. What *did you block the rear wheels* with?
2. How ______________________________?
3. What ______________________________ on?
4. How many ______________________________?
5. What ______________________________?
6. Why ______________________________?

C Match the answers to the questions in **B**. Use complete sentences.

a. Tools and know-how – b. *Grease* – c. Eight – d. Wooden blocks – e. *Lug wrench* – f. *Jack stands*

wobble – Wackeln
hand brake – Handbremse
raise, v – anheben
support, v – (ab-)stützen
wheel rim – Felge
drive shaft – Antriebswelle
grease – Fett, Schmiere
lug wrench – Kreuzschlüssel
jack stand – Unterstellbock

UNIT 8

Active and passive safety

Safety plays an important role in the design of a car. Active safety *features* are those which help drivers *avoid* accidents. Passive safety features help drivers and passengers *stay alive* and *uninjured* in a crash.

feature – Eigenschaft, Merkmal
avoid, v – vermeiden
stay alive – am Leben bleiben
uninjured – unverletzt
device – Vorrichtung
headrest – Kopfstütze
belt pre-tensioner – Gurtstraffer
tyre – Reifen
electronic stability program – elektronisches Stabilitätsprogramm

A Look at the safety *devices* and systems shown below. Which are active features and which are passive ones?

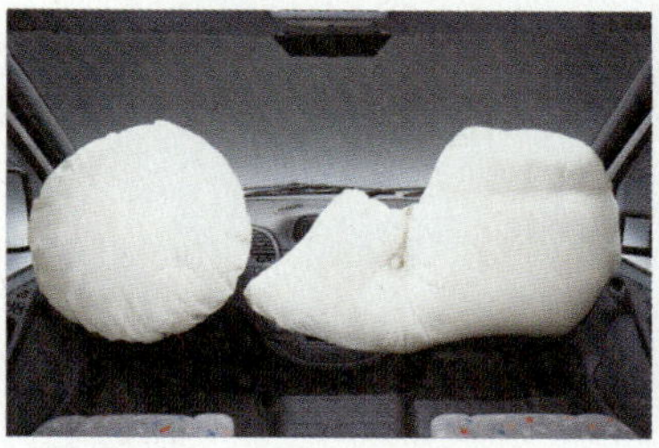

airbag

headrest

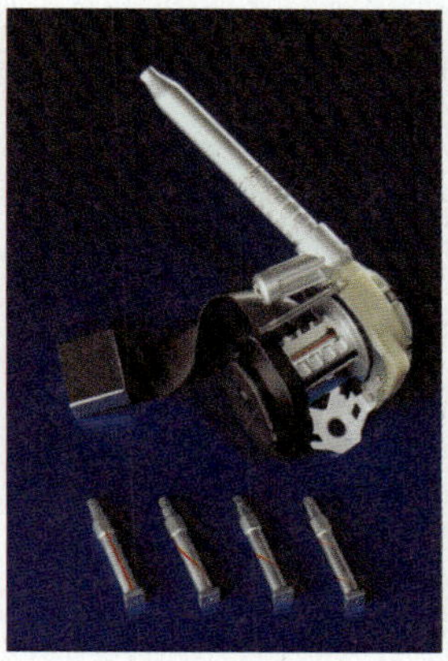

belt pre-tensioner

seat belt

tyre

anti-lock braking system

electronic stability control program

traction control

B Which of the above features …

1. helps you stop shorter and maintain steering control while *braking*?
2. improves traction and *directional* stability on *slippery* roads?
3. helps stabilize a vehicle's *handling* when it is pushed to the limit?
4. tightens the belt when it is *slack*?
5. prevents the *occupant's* head from hitting the *dashboard, steering wheel* or *windscreen*?
6. *minimizes whiplash*?

traction control – Antriebsschlupfregelung
brake, v – bremsen
directional – richtungs-
slippery – rutschig
handling – Fahrverhalten
slack – schlaff
occupant – Insasse, Insassin
dashboard – Armaturenbrett
steering wheel – Lenkrad
windscreen – Windschutzscheibe
minimize, v – minimieren
whiplash – Schleudertrauma

1 Requesting, offering, suggesting and asking permission

request, v – bitten
offer, v – anbieten
suggest, v – vorschlagen
ask permission – um Erlaubnis bitten
suggestion – Vorschlag
brake disk – Bremsscheibe
supervision – Aufsicht
similar – ähnlich

A In pairs, write down what phrases you use for asking someone to do something, offering to help someone, making a suggestion and asking someone for permission. Think of as many phrases as possible.

B Mike and Sarah are in the workshop removing the front *brake discs* of a car under *supervision*. Listen to the dialogue. Write down the phrases the speakers use for requesting, offering to help, suggesting and asking permission.
Put the phrases into suitable categories.
Are they *similar* to your phrases from **A**?

requests	offers	suggestions	asking permission

C Listen to the dialogue again. Write down how they replied to the offers, suggestions and requests.

D The words in the sentences below are not in the correct order.
Rearrange them.

1. please / to / wear / I'd / masks / you / like / , / .

___

2. screws / could / remove / think / you / Do / the / you / ?

___

3. I / all right / bolts / it / the / unscrew / if / Is / ?

___

4. you / very / kind / of / That's / .

___

5. can't / now / open / you / I'm / it / afraid / .

____

6. up / I / tools / tidy / Shall / the / ?

____

7. thanks / manage / it / No / , / can / I / .

____

8. I / May / now / break / a / take / ?

____

E Write a dialogue. Continue the dialogue in 1B between Steffen Berger, Mike and Sarah. Use the expressions learned and the technical terms in the box on the right.

remove rust and *burrs*
place disc over *hub*
insert Allen-head screws
place caliper over disc
install *retaining* bolts
tighten to *specified torque*

2 Acronyms

A Work in pairs. Below are 14 acronyms („Abkürzungen") and their English meanings. What are they in German? Use a dictionary if necessary.

1. ATF – Automatic Transmission Fluid
2. BDC – Bottom Dead Centre
3. DI – Direct Injection
4. EPHS – Electrically Powered Hydraulic Steering
5. ESP – Electronic Stability Control Program
6. FWD – Four-Wheel Drive
7. GPS – Global Positioning System
8. LED – Light Emitting Diode
9. LHD – Left-Hand Drive
10. MOT – Ministry of Transport*
11. SRS – Supplementary Restraint System
12. TC – Traction Control
13. TDC – Top Dead Centre
14. VIN – Vehicle Identification Number

* TÜV – Technischer Überwachungsverein

B Do you know any other acronyms? What do they stand for?

I'd like you to … – Ich hätte gern, dass du / ihr …
Would you like me to …? – Möchtest du, dass ich …?
be short of time – wenig Zeit haben
brake caliper – Bremssattel
brake pad – Bremsbelag
Take your time! – Lass dir Zeit!
rust – Rost
starve, v – verhungern
canteen – Kantine
I put my foot in it. – Ich trete ins Fettnäpfchen
burr – Grat
hub – Nabe
insert, v – hineinstecken
Allen-head screw – Imbusschraube
retaining bolt – Befestigungsbolzen, -schraube
specified – vorgegeben
torque – Dreh-, Anzugsmoment

3 Spot on safety

A Read the following newspaper article. *According to* the text, what is the function of a seat in a future crash?

There are many safety features in today's vehicles, including high-performance *adaptive* airbags, side airbags and *side curtain airbags*, seat belt pre-tensioners and belt *force limiters* and crash-optimized car body structures. Safety experts believe that passive safety technology has now been *exploited* and that further *advances* will require new concepts.

Preventive occupant safety is a new concept based on the fact that in two thirds of all traffic accidents there is a long *interval* between the time when the driver recognizes that an accident is going to happen, and the *impact* itself. The *researchers* believe new technology can activate the vehicle's protection systems during this interval.

In a future vehicle, the new occupant protection systems would go into action when sensors in the car *detect* that the vehicle is on a *collision* course with another vehicle. Even before the driver has time to react and apply the brakes, the seat belts will *tense* and *restrain* the driver's and passengers' bodies, preventing them from moving forward during the braking and *ensuring* a safe seating position. At the same time, the seat *cushions* of the front passenger and rear seats will automatically *tilt* to the rear. Also, at the same time the *door panels* will move into the car's interior and *mould* themselves around the occupants' *hips* like protective *shields*.

Research engineers are planning a "thinking car" that is able to recognize its *surroundings*: This means not only the road ahead or other vehicles, but also traffic lights, road signs and *pedestrians*. The cars of the future will be able to *monitor* traffic and, if necessary, take accident prevention measures by themselves.

according to – nach, laut
adaptive – anpassungsfähig
side (curtain) airbag – Seitenairbag
force limiter – Kraftbegrenzer
exploit, v – ausbeuten, ausnutzen
advances – Fortschritte
preventive – vorbeugend
interval – Zeitabstand
impact – Aufprall
researcher – Forscher/in
detect, v – erkennen, ermitteln
collision – Zusammenstoß
tense, v – (sich) straffen
restrain, v – zurückhalten
ensure, v – sicher stellen
cushion – Sitzkissen
tilt, v – kippen
door panel – Türverkleidung
mould, v – formen
hip – Hüfte
shield – Schutzschild
surroundings – Umgebung
pedestrian – Fußgänger/in
monitor, v – überwachen

B Answer the questions on the text.

1. Why do safety experts believe that new concepts are needed?
2. What fact is the new safety concept based on?
3. When exactly will the seat belts tense in a future crash?
4. What will the "thinking car" be able to do in the future?

C Form small groups. Discuss the ideas mentioned in the article. Are they realistic?

D In small groups come up with a new safety idea for a future car. Write it down in German. Present it to your class in English.

UNIT 9

Transmissions

Automotive technology has *reached* a very high standard today in engine transmission *development*. In the old days transmissions were not *synchronized*, so drivers had to *develop* quite a talent to *change gear* without any *grinding* sound. Later transmissions with synchronizers were *designed*, and today automatic transmissions, *especially* with electronic control, have become more and more popular.

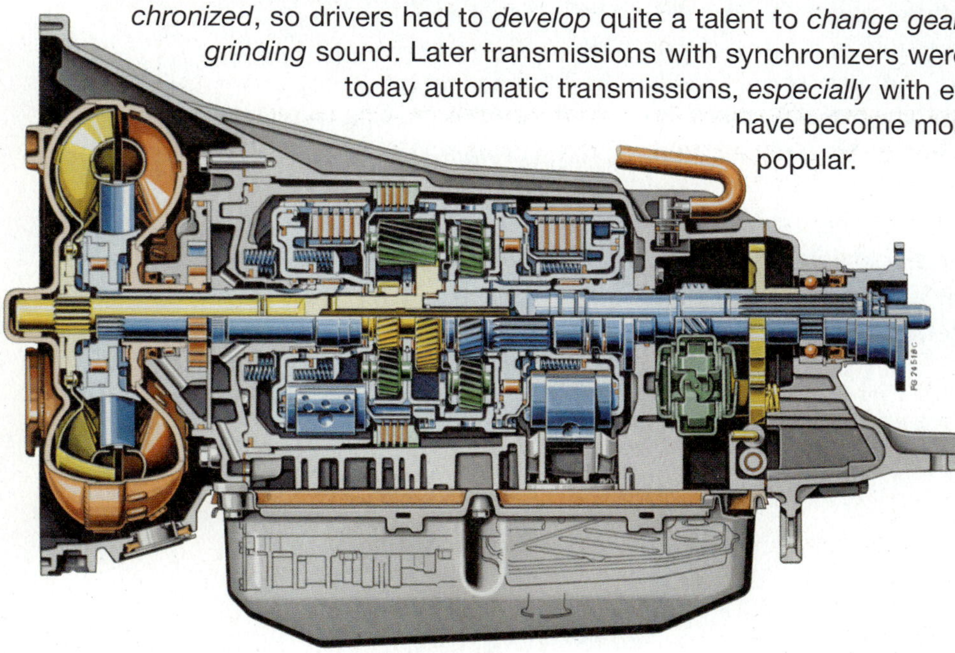

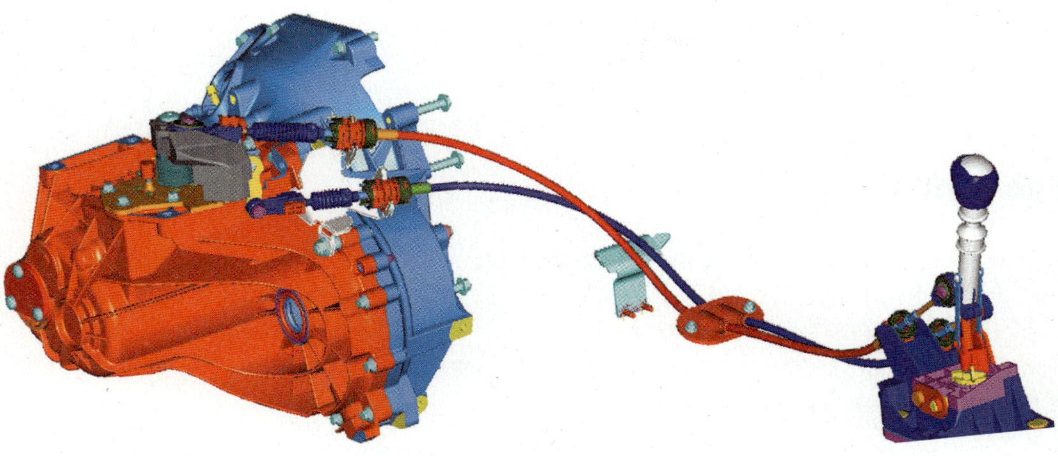

- Which transmission systems have been mentioned in the text above, and which can you see in the pictures?

____

____

____

transmission – Getriebe
reach, v – erreichen
development – Entwicklung
synchronized – synchronisiert
develop, v – entwickeln
change gear – schalten
gear – (Schaltung) Gang
grinding – knirschend
design, v – konstruieren
especially – besonders

1 Manual transmission

Taking driving lessons is not as easy as it sounds, because changing gear is no fun! How does it work? Press down the *clutch* pedal and *shift* the *gear lever* into first gear position. Now *release* the clutch gently while pushing down the *acceleration pedal* at the same time. At the beginning this is rather difficult to do without the engine *stalling*, but after some practice the learner drivers *succeed*, because the *5-speed manual transmissions* on standard cars are synchronized.

clutch – Kupplung
shift, v – bewegen
gear lever – Schalthebel
release, v – loslassen, lösen
acceleration pedal – Gaspedal
stall, v – (Motor) abwürgen
succeed, v – Erfolg haben
5-speed manual transmission – Fünfgangschaltgetriebe
left-hand drive – Linkssteuerung
prefer, v – bevorzugen
nowadays – heutzutage
increase, v – zunehmen
brain – Gehirn
relieve, v – befreien, entlasten
component – Teil, Bestandteil
torque converter – Drehmomentwandler
downstream planetary gearset – Planetengetriebe
control – Steuerung
selector lever – Wählhebel

A How do you change gear in a non-synchronized transmission? Put the steps below in the correct order.

- ☐ Release the clutch gently.
- ☐ Shift the gear lever into first gear position.
- ☐ Push down the acceleration pedal at the same time.
- ☐ Press down the clutch pedal.

B Point out in German what is important to prevent the engine stalling when shifting into first gear. ______________________________

____

2 Automatic transmission

The following text describes a *left-hand drive* car. What is different in a right-hand drive car?

Many drivers *prefer* to use an automatic transmission *nowadays*, because it is easier to start off and you don't need to shift gears.

There is also a safety aspect which is important in times of *increasing* traffic: the left foot, the right hand as well as the *brain* are *relieved* of the task of shifting, so the drivers can pay all their attention to driving.

Modern automatic transmissions generally have five gears and consist of three *components*: the *torque converter*, the *downstream planetary gear set* and the *control*. With the *selector lever* the driver can *engage* the *parking lock*, the *idle speed* and the *reverse gear*. He can also *lock* the lower gears against shifting. If you need to increase speed *rapidly*, engage the kick-down.

However, there is a *disadvantage* in case of an *engine breakdown*. With an automatic transmission the car can't be *towed*, because the hydraulic oil system of the transmission engine isn't on.

A *Label* the illustration with the English words for the planetary gear set.

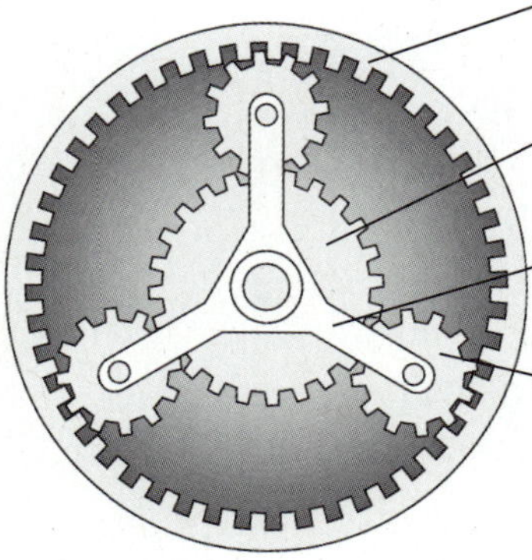

planet gear – ring gear – sun gear – carrier

engage, v – einstellen, (Gang) einlegen
parking lock – Parksperre
idle speed – Leerlauf
reverse gear – Rückwärtsgang
lock, v – sperren
rapid(ly) – schnell, rasch
disadvantage – Nachteil
engine breakdown – Motorschaden
tow, v – (Auto) abschleppen
label,v – beschriften
various – verschiedenartig
axle drive – Achsantrieb
four-wheel drive – Vierradantrieb
off-road vehicle – Geländefahrzeug
rear-wheel drive – Hinterradantrieb
dirt road – unbefestigte Straße

B Read or listen to the text in 2 again and point out
1. the features of the selector lever of the automatic transmission.
2. the disadvantage of automatic transmissions.

3 Various axle drives

Mike has just read about the latest *four-wheel drive* car, and he is discussing it with Sarah and Christian.

A Listen to the conversation between Mike, Sarah and Christian. Which axle drives are they talking about?

B Listen to the conversation again. Match the *advantages* and disadvantages below with the *corresponding* axle drive.

higher *fuel consumption* / good driving safety / good for off-road driving / no skidding when the car speeds up / danger of skidding / better driving safety / more wear and tear / less wear of drive shafts / higher wear of drive shafts and joints / engage automatically / better steering / good on slippery roads

icy – vereist, eisglatt
road conditions – Straßenverhältnisse
front-wheel drive – Frontantrieb
skid, v – schleudern
wear out, v – (sich) abnutzen
joint – Gelenk
consume, v – verbrauchen
wear and tear – Verschleiß, Abnutzung
advantage – Vorteil
corresponding – entsprechend
fuel consumption – Kraftstoffverbrauch
garage – Autowerkstatt

4 Spot on grammar

Present perfect tense (Vollendete Gegenwart)

Das **present perfect** wird bei regelmäßigen Verben mit **have** oder **has** + regelmäßige 3. Verbform (**ed**-Endung) gebildet, bei unregelmäßigen Verben mit **have** oder **has** + 3. Verbform (**taken**)

Das **present perfect** wird verwendet:
- bei Handlungen in der Vergangenheit ohne Zeitangabe
- bei Handlungen mit Zeitbestimmungen wie **so far, this week, this year ...**
- bei Handlungen, die in der Vergangenheit begonnen haben, aber noch nicht abgeschlossen sind, wobei **for** bei Zeiträumen (**2 hours / 3 days**) und **since** bei Zeitpunkten (**February / 1999**) benutzt wird.

He has tightened the bolts and nuts.

They haven't made the process plans so far.

She has lived in Stuttgart for 15 years.

I have studied this new technology since I left school.

A Complete the following sentences. Use the present perfect.

1. (like) We ______________ always _______________ sports cars.
2. (build) The company _______________________ a very good new limousine.
3. (drive) ____________ you ever ________________ a four-wheel drive car?
4. (not employ) This garage _______________________ any apprentices before.
5. (be) How long ____________ you _______________ at this college?

B Complete the interview between Sarah and Mike and Peter Stott, the editor of the magazine "Voice of trainees". Use **since** or **for**.

Peter: How long have you been with CarFit?

Sarah: Well, I've been with CarFit ① ______ about 6 months now, ② ______ leaving school in the United States.

Mike: And I've been here ③ ______ I started work.

Peter: What has it been like so far?

Mike: I've been doing a lot of turning and milling ④ ______ the last few weeks.

Sarah: I started in the Body Shop right away before I moved to the service department. I've learned how to deal with customers ⑤ ______ I started work.

Peter: I see. What made you decide to work in the automobile industry?

Sarah: I've been interested in cars ever ⑥ ______ I went to a car race when I was ten.

Mike: And I've had the chance of helping out at a *garage* every Saturday ⑦ ______ the last three months.

UNIT 10

Assembly and inspection

Many modern luxury models include the following standard features.

1. vehicle navigation system

2. cup holder

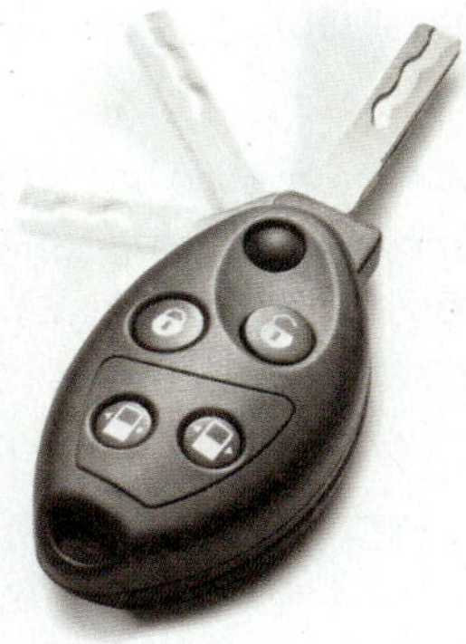

3. *remote* entry system

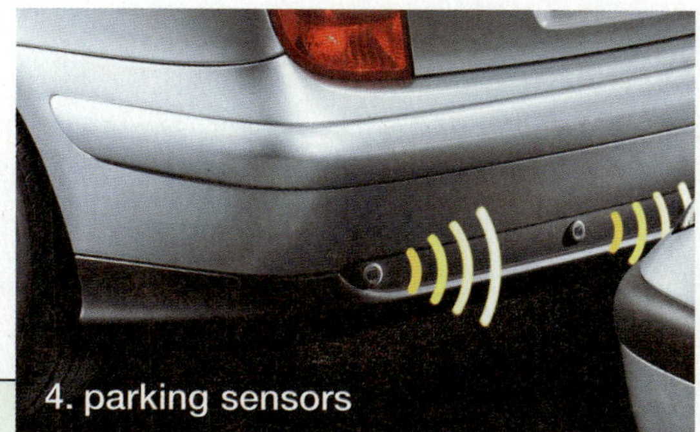

4. parking sensors

driver's airbag	ESP, electronic stability program
map reading lights	*energy absorbing steering column*
rear window power *sunshade*	remote fuel door *release*
colour-keyed body side mouldings	*anti-theft* system
side impact airbag	*tinted* reflective glass
central locking system	rain sensing wipers
cigarette lighter	
cruise control	

A In a small group divide the features into three categories. Put at least five features into each category. The categories are:

1. *essential* in any modern vehicle, a must
2. useful to have, but could do without it
3. *unnecessary*, a *waste* of money, really

Essential	Useful	Unnecessary

B When you have reached agreement in your group try to reach a consensus in the class.

inspection – Kontrolle, Prüfung
remote(-controlled) – ferngesteuert
sunshade – Sonnenblende
colour-keyed – farblich abgestimmt
body side moulding – Flankenschutzleiste
cruise control – Geschwindigkeitsregler, Tempomat
energy absorbing steering column – Sicherheitslenksäule
release – Entriegelung
anti-theft – gegen Diebstahl
tinted – (Glas) getönt
essential – (unbedingt) notwendig
unnecessary – unnötig
waste – Verschwendung

1 From assembly to final inspection

A Read each of the seven sections carefully and put the text into the correct sequence. Number the paragraphs.

[1] The assembly area conducts the final application of parts to complete the vehicle. It is usually the largest and most *labour intensive* area of the plant.

☐ The marriage of the body and chassis takes place on the final line. The body is fitted onto *rubber* mounts as it is joined to the freshly finished chassis. Much of the remaining work involves systems that are shared by both body and chassis, such as the installation of steering and *suspension* components.

☐ The assembly area is divided into three operations. The first is the *trim* division. As the vehicle starts on the first line it is completely empty with no assembled parts. It has just been through the Paint Shop and stored in a *high-bay store* waiting for call up.

[3] This area assembles those parts which the customer does not normally see such as *silencer pads* to make the car quieter, interior trim, heating and air conditioning units, and electrical wiring harnesses. The vehicle is *conveyed* on a *skid* through to the chassis area.

☐ Once the wheels and necessary fluids have been added, the vehicle is almost finished. Each body is built for a specific chassis. They both arrive at the marriage station exactly on time and a new vehicle is born.

☐ This process manages the underbody sub-assembly and engine build-up. These parts include the brake and fuel lines, underbody suspension, transmission and axles. The final area is responsible for many customer appearance items such as the instrument panel, seating, *carpeting* and *headliner*, and interior panel trim.

[7] Processes completed after the marriage of body and chassis are: tyre installation, final fluid fills such as power steering fluid, radiator fluid, window washer and fuel. Final inspection and quality testing are carried out at the very end of the process to make sure the customer is getting a top class product.

B Listen to the text and check the correct sequence.

C Decide whether the following statements are true or false.

true	false	
☐	☐	1. The vehicle goes straight from the Paint Shop to the Assembly Shop.
☐	☐	2. Carpeting is installed after the wiring harness.
☐	☐	3. The marriage takes place after the air conditioning is installed.
☐	☐	4. Final inspection is performed throughout the process.

labour intensive – arbeitsintensiv
rubber – Gummi
suspension – Aufhängung
trim – Innenausstattung
high-bay store – Hochregallager
silencer pads – schalldämpfende Füllung
convey, v – befördern
skid – Förderschlitten
carpeting – Bodenbelag
headliner – Himmel

2 Checking the brakes

•  An MOT inspector is talking to a group of trainees about checking the vehicle's brakes. Read the checklist carefully. Then listen and tick ✔ the checks he refers to.

worn to excess – vollständig abgenutzt
mountings – Aufhängung
breakage – Bruch(-schaden)
contamination – Verunreinigung
assignment – Aufgabe, Auftrag
supervisor – Aufseher/in, Aufsicht
reduce, v – verringern, reduzieren
mediate, v – (Inhalte) vermitteln
stock – (Material-)Bestand

1. Check the footbrake so that it does not go down to the floor.	
2. Check that the pedal rubber on the footbrake is not *worn to excess*.	
3. The *mountings* are checked for corrosion.	
4. The master cylinder and servo unit are checked with the engine running.	
5. The servo unit is checked to ensure it is operating correctly.	
6. All visible metal or flexible brake pipes are checked for corrosion, *breakage* or leaks.	
7. Discs and drums are checked for condition and *contamination*.	
8. Mechanical parts are checked electronically.	
9. The condition of the brake pads is checked.	
10. The brake compensating valve beneath the car is inspected for fluid leaks.	
11. The performance of the front and rear brakes is checked using special equipment.	

3 Avoiding waste

While on a job *assignment* in the Final Assembly area a *supervisor* informs the trainees how to avoid and *reduce* waste in the manufacturing facility. Christian has to *mediate* for Sarah and Mike and tell them what has been said.

• Take the role of Christian.

1. Reduziere Materialbestände zwischen allen Arbeitsschritten.

____

2. Produziere nur, was gebraucht wird und wenn es gebraucht wird.

____

3. Vermeide Zeitverschwendung und unnötige Bewegung im Arbeitsprozess.

____

4 Confusing words

- Fill the gaps in the sentences below with a suitable form of the word in the box. Be careful, some words are used more than once.

install (to put in and connect up)
assemble (to put parts together)
mount (to put one part on top of another)
join (to bring together)
demount (to take one part off another)
disassemble (to take something apart)

1. There are many different ___joining___ technologies: spot-welding, *bonding* and *riveting* are just some.
2. After repair the engine is ______________ onto the sub-frame by a *hoist*.
3. The mechanic ______________ the gearbox to find the damaged *cog-wheel*.
4. The front seats were sub-______________ at the suppliers and then transported to the ______________ plant.
5. The *seat pan* was ______________ onto the seat rails and they were ______________ together with steel bolts.
6. Before the carpeting is put in, the wiring harness has to be ______________ into the vehicle.
7. First the wheels have to be ______________ before the tyres can be changed.

5 Spot on safety

- Read the following safety regulations about *fire extinguishers*. Complete the text with the missing words.

requirements
obstructed
depends
ensure
fully
installed
shall

Fire extinguishers shall be ① ______________ in all shop areas.

The number of extinguishers ② ______________ on the size and layout of the facility.

Fire extinguishers ③ ______________ meet the following ④ ____________________________:

- be kept ⑤ ____________ charged and in their designated area.
- not be ⑥ ________________________ from view.
- be visually inspected at least monthly to ⑦ ______________ that they do not have corrosion or other impairments.

bonding – Kleben
riveting – Vernieten
hoist – Hebezug, Kettenzug
cog-wheel – Zahnrad
seat pan – Sitzwanne
fire extinguisher – Feuerlöscher
obstruct, v – versperren
depend, v – abhängen

UNIT 11

Servicing

When Steffen Berger comes into his office after lunch on Monday he has got this message on his *answering machine*:

- Listen to the phone call. Note down the problem Sarah and Christian have.

Christian: Service station.
S. Berger: Hello. Is that you, Christian?
Christian: Yes. Oh, Herr Berger. Thanks for ringing me back. Sarah and I've got to do the servicing on Ms Forster's car.
S. Berger: So what's the problem?
Christian: Well, while doing all the check-ups *required* in the servicing *manual* for this service we've found that one *fuel line injection nozzle* is faulty.
S. Berger: I can't see any problem so far. Just exchange it for a new one.
Christian: Well, of course we've already done that. But during the test run the injection pump turned out to be faulty, too. Now Sarah thinks that it will be quite expensive to exchange the pump.
S. Berger: Oh, yes, a new pump won't be cheap. But these injection pumps aren't repaired any more nowadays, you know.
Christain: That's what I thought, too. So we'll have to exchange the pump.
S. Berger: Yes, I'm afraid you'll have to. But perhaps it would be a nice idea to phone Ms Forster. Inform her and ask her if she *agrees*.
Christian: OK. I'll ask Sarah to do that because she's *experienced* in dealing with customers.
S. Berger: All right. Is there anything else I can do for you, Christian?
Christian: No, thanks a lot, that's it for the moment, I guess.
Bye-bye.
S. Berger: Bye.

service / servicing – Kundendienst
answering machine – Anrufbeantworter
ring back, v – zurückrufen
customer – Kunde, Kundin
required – erforderlich, verlangt
manual – Handbuch
fuel line – Kraftstoffleitung
injection nozzle – Einspritzdüse
agree, v – zustimmen
be experienced – Erfahrung haben

1 Customer care

When customers have their cars regularly serviced they are sometimes *surprised* about the *invoice* and the cost of spare parts and repair. They would often *appreciate* a rough *estimate* before the work is done.

surprise, v – überraschen
invoice – Rechnung
appreciate, v – zu schätzen wissen
estimate – Kostenvoranschlag

• Work in pairs. Prepare Sarah's phone call with Ms Forster with the help of the words and phrases listed below. Present the telephone dialogue to the class.

Sarah

CarFit, service station / almost / like to inform about an extra repair job / not at all / fuel injection pump has to be replaced / it'll cost a little extra / about another €350 / not possible / nowadays these parts are only replaced / …

Ms Forster

speaking / servicing finished / what is it / problematic / sounds expensive / how much / no other way / repair or exchange it for a second-hand one / if you say so, you're the expert / …

2 Support service

Nowadays it is not *unusual* for garages, which regularly service their customers' cars, to support their customers by *reminding* them when the next service is *due*. They either ring them or send a letter, a fax or an e-mail.

A Read the following letter. Note down all important facts and data in German.

CarFit Service & Repair Ltd • Siemens Str. 14-16 • 70173 Stuttgart
phone: +49 (0)711 / 54 61 54 0
fax: +49 (0)711 / 54 61 54 12

Ms M. Forster
Habichtweg 13
70199 Stuttgart

1 July 2003

Date of servicing: 15 July 2003

Dear Ms Forster

We would like to remind you that the next service is due on 15 July 2003.
We would appreciate it if you could make an appointment with us at your earliest convenience.

We look forward to hearing from you soon.

Yours sincerely
Sarah Jackson
Sarah Jackson for Steffen Berger
Service Station

B Schreiben Sie eine E-Mail auf Englisch, in der Sie die Kundin Margaret Ryan an den nächstfälligen Kundendiensttermin ihres Fahrzeugs am 7. April erinnern. Folgende Daten sollten in dem Schreiben enthalten sein:
Absender: s.jackson@carfit-mail.de
Adresse: m.ryan@gmx.de
Datum, Betreff, Anrede, Mailinhalt, Schluss,
Fußnote mit Namen der Schreiberin, Firmenadresse

support service – Kundenbetreuung
unusual – ungewöhnlich
remind, v – erinnern
due – fällig
Ltd (limited) – GmbH
appointment – Termin
at your earliest convenience – möglichst bald
look forward to, v – sich freuen auf

CarFit Service & Repair Ltd
Siemens Str. 14-16
70173 Stuttgart
phone: +49 (0)711 / 54 61 54 0
fax: +49 (0)711 / 54 61 54 12
e-mail: s.jackson@carfit-mail.de

3 Useful words

- In each of the following words from this Unit two vowels (a, e, i, o, u) are missing. Fill them in.

1. q_ _stion	5. f_ _lty	9. id_ _	13. exper_ _nced
2. man_ _l	6. ch_ _p	10. d_ _l	14. apprec_ _te
3. f_ _l	7. q_ _te	11. d_ _	15. app_ _ntment
4. inject_ _n	8. rep_ _r	12. unus_ _l	16. inv_ _ce

4 Spot on grammar

will-future (Zukunft mit 'will')
Die Zukunft mit **will** drückt die Bereitschaft und Entschlossenheit aus, etwas zu tun. Sie wird auch benutzt für eine spontane Entscheidung und ein Versprechen. Nach **will** steht das Verb immer unverändert im Infinitiv (Grundform). Die Kurzform wird mit **'ll** gebildet, in der Verneinung mit **won't**.

*I'll **do** my best to finish the work on time.*
*Just a minute, **I'll ask** him!*

• Complete the following sentences. Use the will-future.

1. Mike ______________ his very best to do a good job. (do)
2. We ________________ clock out before we go. (have to)
3. The customer ________________ the next date of service. (not forget)
4. The trainees all hope the instruction __________________ by about 2 p.m. (be over)
5. The customer expects that his car ___________ finished by 5 p.m. (be)
6. After his training Mike _________________ his instructor's help any more. (not need)
7. Wait a minute! I ____________ you. (help)
8. Steffen Berger is sure that he _______________ the servicing by four this afternoon. (finish)

5 Old and new

• Look at the white Triumph (year of manufacture 1962), the red Triumph Spitfire (1977) and the modern Porsche 911 Carrera. Which of these cars would you prefer to drive? Give reasons. Think of comfort / fun / technology / appearance / …

UNIT 12

Job application and interview

application – Bewerbung
interview – Bewerbungsgespräch
advertisement (ad) – Anzeige
vacancy – freie Stelle

1 Looking at job advertisements

Although they have not finished their training yet, Christian and Sarah are looking at job ads in the newspaper and in the Internet where they find some interesting *vacancies.*

A Read the two advertisements below. Say where the jobs are offered.

File Number: 110 – 05

International garage for service and engine *tune-ups* in Switzerland requires
2 Electronics / Mechatronics Technicians
practically-minded and open to new *challenges*
You will work in an international team with mechanics and electronic technicians.
Qualifications: One to two years' *experience* in Electronics / Mechantronics (or *equivalent*); Basic CAD skills are *desirable* but not essential
Language required: fluent German, good English
Salary: negotiable

Applications in English to:
SICS – **S**wiss **I**nternational **C**ar **S**ervice
The Staff Manager
Basler Weg 101 – 103
8803 Rueschlikon / Switzerland

File Number: 12 – 03 W

Automotive Mechanic
Graduation from high school, *vocational school* or with work experience as an automotive mechanic. Experience with *heavy-duty equipment* is desirable but not essential. *Driver's license* and acceptable driving record required. Must be *dependable*, punctual and *prepared* to work second shifts from 12.30 p.m. to 9 p.m.
10% extra *pay* for all second shift hours. *CV* and photo are required with the application.
Pay: $25000 p.a. (per annum)

Apply to **CarTech Ltd** • 132 Rock Road
Wood End, Birmingham • Alabama, 35203 • USA

tune-up – (Motor) Tuning
practically-minded – praktisch denkend
challenge – Herausforderung
experience – Erfahrung
equivalent – gleichwertig
desirable – erwünscht
salary – Gehalt
negotiable: The salary is negotiable. – Über das Gehalt kann verhandelt werden.
graduation – Abschluss
vocational school – Berufsschule
heavy-duty equipment – Hochleistungsausrüstung
driver's license – (US) Führerschein
dependable – zuverlässig
be prepared – bereit sein
pay – Lohn
CV (curriculum vitae) – Lebenslauf

B Which of the jobs offered would they take? Give reasons.

C Which job would interest **you** more? Give reasons.

2 A letter of application

either … or – entweder … oder
job centre – Arbeitsamt
careers officer – Berufsberater/in
résumé – (US) Lebenslauf
most recent – neuester, letzter
primary school – Grundschule
supplier – Lieferant
finals – Abschlussprüfung
quality assurance – Qualitätssicherung
knowledge – Wissen
ability – Fähigkeit
consider, v – berücksichtigen

A Read the following text.
What can you do in order to find a job?

When you are looking for a job there are different ways of finding one. *Either* you check the advertisements in a newspaper, ask a friend *or* go to the *job centre* and ask the *careers officer* for help. Quite an attractive and popular way is the Internet, where you can get a lot of information about the company that offers the job.
But no matter which way you choose: If you apply, you will always have to write a letter of application and a CV (or a *résumé* in American English) with your personal history in short. And finally, if all goes well you should be prepared for an interview with questions such as "Why do you want to work at our company?" or "Why do you think you are qualified for this job?"

B Christian has not finished his training yet so he cannot apply for a job at the moment. He wants to find out more about applications in English. Listen to the dialogue. Take notes of all the important tips for writing an application.

C Use the following information to write your own letter of application. Think about paragraphs and layout.

> Dear Sir or Madam, I would like to apply for the job as an electrician advertised in the Internet under file number 3002 – 56 B. I have been doing my education and training at VoltTech, a car electrics *supplier*, for the last three years, and have just finished my *finals*. During my training I specialized in CAD tools and *quality assurance* methods. I feel that my technical *knowledge* and my *ability* to speak English are ideal for working in an international company. Thank you for *considering* my application. If you need any further information, please write or call me.
>
> Yours faithfully, ________________________

3 Tips on writing a CV

When you are writing a CV always use a *word processing program*. For a good presentation it is necessary to think of the rules in the box on the next page.

- Read the rules. Should you always include a picture of yourself in a CV? Should you tell the company how much you would like to earn?

- When you apply for a job in Great Britain the CV should not be longer than one or two pages.
- Use good quality paper.
- Write about your own *strengths* and *achievements*.
- Include a photo if required.
- Give the names of two *referees*.
- Never send a CV without a *covering letter*, which includes your address and the date.
- Start with your most recent job during your education and work experience.
- Check your spelling and ask a friend to *double-check* it.
- Include your *salary requirement* only if you are asked to do so.
- Don't ask the company to send back your CV – most companies like to keep it.
- Keep a copy of your own CV and look at it again before your interview.

4 Mike Fisher's CV

A Read the following example of a CV. Did Mike Fisher go to another country to work there?

Name	Mike Fisher
Address	23 Manchester Road, Bolton, BL2 1ER, Great Britain
Place of birth	Manchester
Age	20
Education	1998 – 2002 Bolton Technical College 1992 – 1998 Moorside Comprehensive School, Manchester
Languages	English and German
Work experience *abroad*	CarFit, Stuttgart, Germany: 6 months as an exchange trainee in car manufacturing
Interests	Travelling, CAM, music, *hang gliding*

word processing program – Textverarbeitungsprogramm
strength – Stärke
achievement – (erreichte) Leistung
referee – Person, die als Referenz dient
covering letter – Begleitbrief
double-check, v – noch einmal (über)prüfen
salary requirement – Gehaltsvorstellung
abroad – im / ins Ausland
hang gliding – Drachenfliegen
make up, v – erfinden, sich ausdenken

B Write a CV with your own personal history, or a CV that you are *making up*.

5 Tips for an interview

- Fill in the missing verbs from the box in the following tips for an interview.

wait – look – not chew – talk about – *smile* – not answer – arrive – give – listen

1. ________________ on time or a few minutes earlier.
2. *Smile* ____________ and shake hands firmly.
3. ________________ until you are offered a chair.
4. Always ________________ interested.
5. ________________ true answers to all questions.
6. ________________ questions with "yes" or "no" only.
7. ________________ gum or eat sweets.
8. ________________ to the interviewer carefully and speak clearly.
9. ________________ your success in training or at work.

6 Spot on grammar

If-clause Typ II (Bedingungssatz)
Der mit **if** eingeleitete Bedingungssatz Typ II beschreibt Bedingungen, deren Erfüllung unwahrscheinlich ist. Das Verb steht in der Vergangenheit. Im Hauptsatz steht vor dem Verb **would** oder **could**. Grundregel: **Kein would im if-Satz.**

__If__ you __damaged__ the insulation of this cable, you __would create__ a short-circuit.
You __would have__ an accident __if__ you __went__ at top speed on an icy road.

- Complete the following sentences with the words in brackets.

1. If you ______________ your CV for a job in Great Britain, you __________________ with the most recent position (write / start).
2. If you ____________ somebody to help you, you ___________ him / her to double-check your letter of application (know / can ask).
3. The trainees _______________ working on the project if they _________________ any help from their instructor (stop / not get).
4. The exchange trainees _______________ another year if they _______________ permission from their home company (stay / get).
5. If you ______________ a job in Germany, you ________________ Canada (not find / can try).

Unregelmäßige Verben

Die Formen sind in folgender Reihenfolge aufgeführt:
Grundform (infinitive), **einfache Vergangenheit** (past simple), **3. Form** (past participle).
Bei den mit • bezeichneten Verben sind auch die regelmäßigen Formen möglich.

be, was/were, been	sein
beat, beat, beaten	schlagen, übertreffen
become, became, become	werden
begin, began, begun	anfangen, beginnen
bend, bent, bent	biegen, krümmen
blow, blew, blown	(Sicherung) durchbrennen
break, broke, broken	(zer)brechen, kaputt machen
bring, brought, brought	(heraus)bringen
build, built, built	bauen
• burn, burnt, burnt	(ver)brennen
burst, burst, burst	platzen
buy, bought, bought	kaufen
can, could, –	können
catch, caught, caught	fangen
choose, chose, chosen	aussuchen, wählen
cling, clung, clung	(sich) festhalten
come, came, come	kommen
cost, cost, cost	kosten
countersink, countersank, countersunk	kegelsenken
cut, cut, cut	schneiden; reduzieren
deal, dealt, dealt	sich befassen (mit)
dig, dug, dug	graben
do, did, done	tun, machen
draw, drew, drawn	zeichnen, malen
• dream, dreamt, dreamt	träumen
drink, drank, drunk	trinken
drive, drove, driven	(Auto) fahren
eat, ate, eaten	essen
fall, fell, fallen	fallen
feel, felt, felt	fühlen
fight, fought, fought	kämpfen, bekämpfen
find, found, found	finden
fly, flew, flown	fliegen
forget, forgot, forgotten	vergessen
get, got, got	erhalten, bekommen
give, gave, given	geben
go, went, gone	gehen, fahren
grind, ground, ground	schleifen
grow, grew, grown	wachsen
hang, hung, hung	hängen
have (got), had, had	haben
have to, had to, had to	müssen
hear, heard, heard	hören
hit, hit, hit	schlagen
hold, held, held	halten
hurt, hurt, hurt	(sich) verletzen
keep, kept, kept	(be)halten
know, knew, known	wissen; kennen
lead, led, led	führen
• learn, learnt, learnt	lernen
leave, left, left	verlassen, abfahren
lend, lent, lent	leihen
let, let, let	lassen
lie, lay, lain	liegen
lose, lost, lost	verlieren
make, made, made	machen, anfertigen
mean, meant, meant	bedeuten
meet, met, met	(sich) treffen (mit)
outsell, outsold, outsold	mehr als ... verkaufen
pay, paid, paid	(be)zahlen
put, put, put	setzen, legen, stellen
read, read, read	lesen
ride, rode, ridden	reiten; (Motorrad) fahren
ring, rang, rung	läuten, klingeln
run, ran, run	laufen
say, said, said	sagen
see, saw, seen	sehen
sell, sold, sold	verkaufen
set, set, set	(ein)stellen, festlegen
send, sent, sent	senden, schicken
shake, shook, shaken	schütteln
show, showed, shown	zeigen
shoot, shot, shot	schießen
shut, shut, shut	schließen
sit, sat, sat	sitzen
sleep, slept, slept	schlafen
slide, slid, slid	schieben, rutschen
speak, spoke, spoken	sprechen
• speed, sped, sped	jagen, flitzen
• spell, spelt, spelt	buchstabieren
spend, spent, spent	verbringen; (Geld) ausgeben
spring, sprang, sprung	federn; auslösen
stand, stood, stood	stehen
steal, stole, stolen	stehlen
stick, stuck, stuck	kleben
sweep, swept, swept	fegen
swim, swam, swum	schwimmen
take, took, taken	(mit)nehmen
teach, taught, taught	unterrichten
tear, torn, torn	zerreißen
tell, told, told	erzählen
think, thought, thought	denken, meinen
throw, threw, thrown	werfen
understand, understood, understood	verstehen
wake, woke, woken	(auf)wecken
wear, wore, worn	(Kleidung) tragen
wear out, wore out, worn out	sich abnutzen
win, won, won	gewinnen
write, wrote, written	schreiben

Alphabetische Wortliste

Die Übersetzungen beziehen sich auf den jeweiligen Kontext in der angegebenen Unit / Übung.
Nach der Lautschrift finden Sie Kürzel, die die Fundstelle angeben, z. B. 10/2A (Unit 10 Übung 2A).

Abkürzungen und Symbole

*	unregelmäßige Verbform	s.o.	someone (jemand)
HV	Hörverstehensübung	s.th.	something (etwas)
US	amerikanisches Englisch	v	Verb (Zeitwort)
S	Starter- bzw. Auftakt-Seite		

Phonetic alphabet – Lautschrift
[:] bedeutet, dass der vorangehende Laut lang ist
['] bedeutet, dass die folgende Silbe eine Hauptbetonung erhält
[ˌ] bedeutet, dass die folgende Silbe eine Nebenbetonung erhält
[‿] bedeutet, dass die beiden Laute miteinander verbunden werden

[iː] meet ['miːt]
[ɑː] father ['fɑːðə]
[ɔː] morning [mɔːnɪŋ]
[uː] blue [bluː]
[ɜː] Germany ['dʒɜːmənɪ]

[ɪ] in [ɪn]
[e] yes [jes]
[æ] thanks [θæŋks]
[ʌ] much [mʌtʃ]
[ɒ] what [wɒt]
[ʊ] good [gʊd]
[ə] number ['nʌmbə]

[eɪ] name [neɪm]
[aɪ] my [maɪ]
[ɔɪ] point [pɔɪnt]
[əʊ] phone [fəʊn]
[aʊ] now [naʊ]
[ɪə] beer [bɪə]
[eə] where [weə]
[ʊə] tourist ['tʊərɪst]

[p] park [pɑːk]
[b] bye [baɪ]
[t] taxi ['tæksɪ]
[d] dinner ['dɪnə]
[k] coffee ['kɒfɪ]
[g] good [gʊd]
[tʃ] church [tʃɜːtʃ]
[dʒ] job [dʒɒb]
[f] fine [faɪn]
[v] very ['verɪ]
[θ] thanks [θæŋks]
[ð] this [ðɪs]

[s] son [sʌn]
[z] is [ɪz]
[ʃ] she [ʃiː]
[ʒ] television ['telɪˌvɪʒn]
[h] he [hiː]
[m] my [maɪ]
[n] now [naʊ]
[ŋ] evening ['iːvnɪŋ]
[l] like [laɪk]
[r] room [rʊm]
[w] we [wiː]
[j] yes [jes]

A

ability [ə'bɪlətɪ]	12/2C Fähigkeit
abroad [ə'brɔːd]	12/4A im / ins Ausland
absorb, v [əb'zɔːb]	5/1A aufnehmen
acceleration pedal [əkˌselə'reɪʃn ˌpedl]	9/1 Gaspedal
accept, v [ək'sept]	5/2 annehmen
according to [ə'kɔːdɪŋ tʊ]	8/3A nach, laut
achievement [ə'tʃiːvmənt]	12/3 (erreichte) Leistung
adaptive [ə'dæptɪv]	8/3A anpassungsfähig
add, v [æd]	5/1A hinzufügen
adhesive [əd'hiːsɪv]	4/S Klebstoff
adjustable [ə'dʒʌstəbl]	4/1A verstellbar
adjustable wrench [əˌdʒʌstəbl 'rentʃ]	1/S Rollgabelschlüssel
advances [əd'vɑːnsɪz]	8/3A Fortschritte
advantage [əd'vɑːntɪdʒ]	9/3B Vorteil
advertisement (ad) [əd'vɜːtɪsmənt] [æd]	12/1 Anzeige
agree, v [ə'griː]	11/S zustimmen
air filter ['eə ˌfɪltə]	7/S Luftfilter
Allen-head screw ['ælənhed ˌskruː]	8/1E Imbusschraube, Innensechskantschraube
alternating current (AC) [ˌɒltəneɪtɪŋ 'kʌrənt]	6/1A Wechselstrom
angle grinder ['æŋgl ˌgraɪndə]	1/S Winkelschleifer
answering machine ['ɑːnsərɪŋ məˌʃiːn]	11/S Anrufbeantworter
anti-lock braking system (ABS) [ˌæntɪlɒk 'breɪkɪŋ ˌsɪstəm] [ˌeɪbiː'es]	6/S Antiblockiersystem
anti-theft [ˌæntɪ'θeft]	10/S gegen Diebstahl
A-pillar ['eɪ ˌpɪlə]	5/S A-Säule
A-pillar cross member ['eɪ ˌpɪlə 'krɒs ˌmembə]	5/S Querträger unter Windlauf
application [ˌæplɪ'keɪʃn]	12/1 Bewerbung
apply, v [ə'plaɪ]	5/1A auftragen
appointment [ə'pɔɪntmənt]	11/2A Termin
appreciate, v [ə'priːʃɪeɪt]	6/1C-HV dankbar sein für; zu schätzen wissen
apprentice [ə'prentɪs]	1/1 Lehrling
ask permission [ˌɑːsk pə'mɪʃn]	8/1 um Erlaubnis bitten
assemble, v [ə'sembl]	4/S zusammenbauen
assembly [ə'semblɪ]	1/S Montage
assignment [ə'saɪnmənt]	10/3 Aufgabe, Auftrag
at your earliest convenience [ət jɔːr‿ɜːlɪəst kən'viːnɪəns]	11/2A möglichst bald
automotive [ˌɔːtə'məʊtɪv]	6/S Kfz-
avoid, v [ə'vɔɪd]	8/S vermeiden
axle drive ['æksəl ˌdraɪv]	9/3 Achsantrieb

B

backfire, v [ˌbæk'faɪə]	7/2A knallen (bei Fehlzündung), fehlzünden
basic ['beɪsɪk]	6/1 grundlegend
battery ['bætərɪ]	6/2 Batterie
be* available [bɪ‿ə'veɪləbl]	4/1A zur Verfügung stehen
be* corroded [bɪ kə'rəʊdɪd]	6/2 korrodiert sein
be* equipped [bɪ‿ɪ'kwɪpt]	6/S ausgestattet sein
be* experienced [bɪ‿ɪk'spɪərɪənst]	11/S Erfahrung haben
be* prepared [bɪ prɪ'peəd]	12/1A bereit sein
be* responsible for [bɪ rɪ'spɒnsəbl fɔ:]	2/2A verantwortlich sein für
be* short of time [bɪ ˌʃɔ:t əv 'taɪm]	8/1B-HV wenig Zeit haben
bearing ['beərɪŋ]	7/2A Lager
belt pre-tensioner ['belt ˌpri:'tenʃənə]	8/S Gurtstraffer
bench vice ['bentʃ ˌvaɪs]	1/S Bankschraubstock
blow [bləʊ]	5/1A Schlag
blow*, v [bləʊ]	6/2 (Sicherung) durchbrennen
body part ['bɒdɪ ˌpɑ:t]	2/1B-HV Karosserieteil
Body Shop ['bɒdɪ ˌʃɒp]	2/S Produktion, Fertigung
body shell ['bɒdɪ ˌʃel]	3/1 Rohbaukarrosse
body side moulding ['bɒdɪ ˌsaɪd 'məʊldɪŋ]	10/S Flankenschutzleiste
boilersuit ['bɔɪləˌsu:t]	2/4B Overall
bolt [bəʊlt]	4/S Bolzen, Schraube
bond, v [bɒnd]	4/S kleben
bonding ['bɒndɪŋ]	10/4 Kleben
bonnet ['bɒnɪt]	5/S Motorhaube
bottom dead centre (BDC) [ˌbɒtəm ˌded 'sentə] [ˌbi:di:'si:]	7/1 unterer Totpunkt
B-pillar reinforcement ['bi:ˌpɪlə ˌri:ɪn'fɔ:smənt]	5/S B-Säulen-Verstärkung
bracket ['brækɪt]	3/1A Stütze; Halter, Träger
brain [breɪn]	9/2 Gehirn
brake [breɪk]	5/2 Bremse; bremsen
brake caliper ['breɪk‿ˌkælɪpə]	8/1B-HV Bremssattel
brake disk ['breɪk ˌdɪsk]	8/1B Bremsscheibe
brake pad ['breɪk ˌpæd]	8/1B-HV Bremsbelag
brake pipe ['breɪk ˌpaɪp]	8/1 Bremsleitung
brand [brænd]	3/S Marke
breakage ['breɪkɪdʒ]	10/2-HV Bruch(-schaden)
bumper bracket ['bʌmpə ˌbrækɪt]	5/S Stoßfängerträger
burr [bɜ:]	8/1E Grat

C

camshaft ['kæmʃɑ:ft]	7/S Nockenwelle
canteen [kæn'ti:n]	8/1B-HV Kantine
car lift ['kɑ: ˌlɪft]	4/1A Hebebühne
car mechanic ['kɑ: ˌməˌkænɪk]	1/S Kfz-Mechaniker/in
careers officer [kə'rɪəz ˌɒfɪsə]	12/2A Berufsberater/in
carpeting ['kɑ:pɪtɪŋ]	10/1A Bodenbelag
cause [kɔ:z]	7/1 verursachen; Ursache
central locking system [ˌsentrəl‿'lɒkɪŋ ˌsɪstəm]	6/S Zentralverriegelung
centre punch, v ['sentə ˌpʌntʃ]	1/2A körnen
challenge ['tʃælɪndʒ]	12/1A Herausforderung
change gear [ˌtʃeɪndʒ 'gɪə]	9/S schalten
charge, v [tʃɑ:dʒ]	6/1A (Batterie) aufladen
chassis ['ʃæsɪ]	2/1D-HV Chassis, Fahrgestell
circuit diagram ['sɜ:kɪt ˌdaɪəgræm]	6/1C-HV Schaltplan
clamp, v [klæmp]	1/1A (ein)spannen
clock in, v [ˌklɒk 'ɪn]	3/1A (Zeituhr) stempeln
clothing ['kləʊðɪŋ]	2/4A Kleidung
clutch [klʌtʃ]	9/1 Kupplung
coat [kəʊt]	5/1A Schicht; Beschichtung
cog-wheel ['kɒgwi:l]	10/4 Zahnrad
cold chisel [ˌkəuld‿'tʃɪzl]	4/1A Flachmeißel
collision [kə'lɪʒn]	8/3A Zusammenstoß
colour-keyed ['kʌlə ˌki:d]	10/S farblich abgestimmt
column drill ['kɒləm ˌdrɪl]	1/S Ständerbohrmaschine
combination pliers [ˌkɒmbɪ'neɪʃn ˌplaɪəz]	1/S Kombizange
common ['kɒmən]	3/S alltäglich
compare, v [kəm'peə]	6/1A vergleichen
complicated ['kɒmplɪkeɪtɪd]	1/1A kompliziert
component [kəm'pəʊnənt]	9/2 Teil, Bestandteil
compound word [ˌkɒmpaʊnd 'wɜ:d]	7/S zusammengesetztes Wort
compression stroke [kəm'preʃn ˌstrəʊk]	7/1 Verdichtungstakt
conductor [kən'dʌktə]	6/2 (Elektrizität) Leiter
connecting rod [kə'nektɪŋ ˌrɒd]	7/S Pleuel(-stange)
consider, v [kən'sɪdə]	12/2C berücksichtigen
consist of, v [kən'sɪst əv]	2/2A bestehen aus
consume, v [kən'sju:m]	9/3A-HV verbrauchen
consumption [kən'sʌmʃn]	7/2A Verbrauch
contamination [kənˌtæmɪ'neɪʃn]	10/2-HV Verunreinigung
control [kən'trəʊl]	9/2 Steuerung
convert, v [kən'vɜ:t]	7/1 umwandeln
convey, v [kən'veɪ]	10/1A befördern
conveyor [kən'veɪə]	3/1A Förderer; Förderband
corresponding [ˌkɒrɪ'spɒndɪŋ]	9/3B entsprechend
countersink*, v ['kaʊntəsɪŋk]	1/2A kegelsenken
covering letter ['kʌvərɪŋ ˌletə]	12/3 Begleitbrief
cowl cross member [kaʊl 'krɒs ˌmembə]	5/S (US) Querträger unter Windlauf
crankshaft ['kræŋkʃɑ:ft]	7/1 Kurbelwelle
cross member ['krɒs ˌmembə]	5/S Querträger

cruise control ['kru:z kən,trəʊl]	10/S Geschwindikeitsregler
current ['kʌrənt]	6/1A elektrischer Strom
cushion ['kʊʃn]	8/3A Sitzkissen
customer ['kʌstəmə]	11/S Kunde, Kundin
cutting nippers with hand guard ['kʌtɪŋ‿,nɪpəz wɪð 'hænd ,gɑ:d]	6/S Seitenschneider mit Handschutz
CV (curriculum vitae) [,si:'vi:] [kə,rɪkjələm 'vi:taɪ]	12/1A Lebenslauf
cycle ['saɪkl]	7/1 Kreislauf
cylinder head ['sɪlɪndə ,hed]	7/S Zylinderkopf

D

damaged ['dæmɪdʒd]	5/1 beschädigt
dashboard ['dæʃbɔ:d]	8/S Armaturenbrett
dashboard support ['dæʃbɔ:d sə,pɔ:t]	5/S Instrumententräger
deal* with, v ['di:l wɪð]	6/S sich befassen mit
dealer ['di:lə]	2/S Händler
debur, v [,di:'bɜ:]	1/2A entgraten
demount, v [,di:'maʊnt]	4/2 abbauen, abmontieren
dent [dent]	5/1 Beule
dented ['dentɪd]	4/2 verbeult
department [dɪ'pɑ:tmənt]	2/S Abteilung
depend, v [dɪ'pend]	10/5 abhängen
dependable [dɪ'pendəbl]	12/1A zuverlässig
design, v [dɪ'zaɪn]	9/S konstruieren
desirable [dɪ'zaɪrəbl]	12/1A erwünscht
detect, v [dɪ'tekt]	8/3A erkennen, ermitteln
develop, v [dɪ'veləp]	9/S entwickeln
development [dɪ'veləpmənt]	9/S Entwicklung
device [dɪ'vaɪs]	8/S Vorrichtung, Gerät
diameter [daɪ'æmɪtə]	1/2A Durchmesser
die (press) [daɪ] [pres]	2/1B-HV Press-Stempel, -Werkzeug
dip, v [dɪp]	2/1B-HV (ein)tauchen
direct current (DC) [,daɪrekt 'kʌrənt]	6/1A Gleichstrom
directional [daɪ'rekʃənl]	8/S richtungs-
dirt road ['dɜ:t ,rəʊd]	9/3A-HV unbefestigte Straße
disadvantage [,dɪsəd'vɑ:ntɪdʒ]	9/2 Nachteil
disassemble, v [,dɪsə'sembl]	10/4 auseinander nehmen
dispose of, v [dɪ'spəʊz əv]	4/2A entsorgen
door panel ['dɔ: ,pænl]	8/3A Türverkleidung
door sill ['dɔ: ,sɪl]	5/S Türschweller
double-check, v [,dʌbl'tʃek]	12/3 noch einmal (über)prüfen
downstream planetary gearset [,daʊnstri:m ,plænətrɪ 'gɪəset]	9/2 Planetengetriebe
drawer [drɔ:]	1/3-HV Schublade
drill [drɪl]	1/1A bohren; Bohrer
drill chuck ['drɪl ,tʃʌk]	1/1A Bohrfutter
drive shaft ['draɪv ,ʃɑ:ft]	7/4A Antriebswelle
drive train ['draɪv ,treɪn]	7/S Antriebsstrang, Kraftübertragung
driver's license ['draɪvəz laɪsəns]	12/1A (US) Führerschein
driving licence ['draɪvɪŋ ,laɪsəns]	12/1A Führerschein
due [dju:]	11/2A fällig
dust [dʌst]	5/1A Staub

E

e.g. = for example [,i:'dʒi:] [fər‿ɪg'zɑ:mpl]	4/S z. B. (zum Beispiel)
edge [edʒ]	1/2A Kante
either ... or ['aɪðə ... ɔ:]	12/2A entweder ... oder
electronic stability control program (ESP) [,əlektrɒnɪk stə,bɪlətɪ kən'trəʊl ,prəʊgræm] [,i:es'pi:]	8/S elektronisches Stabilitätsprogramm
employee [ɪm'plɔɪi:]	2/S Beschäftigte/r; Mitarbeiter/in
empty ['emtɪ]	6/2 leer
energy absorbing steering column [,enədʒɪ əbzɔ:bɪŋ 'stɪərɪŋ kɒləm]	10/S Sicherheitslenksäule
engage, v [ɪn'geɪdʒ]	9/2 einstellen; (Gang) einlegen
engine ['endʒɪn]	7/S Motor
engine breakdown ['endʒɪn ,breɪkdaʊn]	9/2 Motorschaden, Panne
engine compartment ['endʒɪn kəm,pɑ:tmənt]	3/1A Motorraum
enquiry [ɪn'kwaɪərɪ]	6/1C Anfrage
ensure, v [ɪn'ʃɔ:]	8/3A sicher stellen
equipment [ɪ'kwɪpmənt]	1/1B Ausstattung
equivalent [ɪ'kwɪvələnt]	12/1A gleichwertig
especially [ɪ'speʃəlɪ]	9/S besonders
essential [ɪ'senʃl]	10/S (unbedingt) notwendig
estate car [ɪ'steɪt ,kɑ:]	3/S Kombiwagen
estimate ['estɪmət]	11/1 Kostenvoranschlag
exchange [ɪks'tʃeɪndʒ]	1/1 Austausch
exciting [ɪk'saɪtɪŋ]	6/1A aufregend, interessant
exhaust [ɪg'zɔ:st]	4/1A Auspuff
exhaust manifold [ɪg'zɔ:st ,mænɪfəʊld]	7/S Auspuffkrümmer
exhaust stroke [ɪg'zɔ:st ,strəʊk]	7/1 Ausstoßtakt
expand, v [ɪk'spænd]	7/1 ausdehnen
experience [ɪk'spɪərɪəns]	12/1A Erfahrung
exploit, v [ɪk'splɔɪt]	8/3A ausbeuten, ausnutzen

F

facility [fə'sɪlətɪ]	2/S Einrichtung
faulty ['fɔ:ltɪ]	3/1A fehlerhaft, schadhaft
feature ['fi:tʃə]	8/S Eigenschaft, Merkmal
fender ['fendə]	5/S (US) Kotflügel

file [faɪl]	1/S Feile; feilen
filler ['fɪlə]	5/1A Spachtelmasse
Final Assembly [ˌfaɪnl ə'semblɪ]	2/S Endmontage
finals ['faɪnlz]	12/2C Abschlussprüfung
finishing file ['fɪnɪʃɪŋ ˌfaɪl]	1/2A Schlichtfeile
fire extinguisher ['faɪər‿ɪksˌtɪŋgwɪʃə]	10/5 Feuerlöscher
firewall ['faɪəwɔ:l]	5/S Spritzwand
firm(ly) [fɜ:m] ['fɜ:mlɪ]	5/1A fest
first aid kit [ˌfɜ:st'eɪd ˌkɪt]	4/4-HV Erste-Hilfe-Ausrüstung, Verbandszeug
5-speed manual transmission ['faɪv'spi:d ˌmænjʊəl trænz'mɪʃn]	9/1 Fünfgangschaltgetriebe
fluid ['flu:ɪd]	8/2A Flüssigkeit
flywheel ['flaɪwi:l]	7/S Schwungrad
force limiter ['fɔ:s ˌlɪmɪtə]	8/3A Kraftbegrenzer
force, v [fɔ:s]	7/1 drücken
forward to, v ['fɔ:wəd‿tʊ]	6/1C-HV weiterleiten, -geben an
four-wheel drive [ˌfɔ:wi:l 'draɪv]	9/3 Vierradantrieb
framing station ['freɪmɪŋ ˌsteɪʃn]	3/1A Aufbaustation
front wing [ˌfrʌnt 'wɪŋ]	5/S Vorderkotflügel
front-wheel drive [ˌfrʌntwi:l 'draɪv]	9/3-HV Frontantrieb
fuel [fjʊəl]	6/1B Kraftstoff
fuel consumption ['fjʊəl kənˌsʌmʃn]	9/3B Kraftstoffverbrauch
fuel line ['fjʊəl‿ˌlaɪn]	11/S Kraftstoffleitung
fuse [fju:z]	6/2 Sicherung

G

garage ['gærɑ:ʒ]	9/4B Autowerkstatt
gasket ['gæskɪt]	7/2A Dichtmanschette
gear ['gɪə]	2/4B Ausrüstung; (Schaltung) Gang
gear lever ['gɪə ˌli:və]	9/1 Schalthebel
generate, v ['dʒenəreɪt]	6/1B erzeugen
generator ['dʒenəreɪtə]	6/1A Lichtmaschine
gently ['dʒentlɪ]	5/1A vorsichtig
go* flat [ˌgəʊ 'flæt]	6/2 (Batterie) schwach werden
goggles ['gɒglz]	1/1A Schutzbrille
grade [greɪd]	5/1A Sorte, Grad
graduation ['grædʒʊ'eɪʃn]	12/1A Abschluss
grease [gri:s]	7/4C Fett, Schmiere
grind*, v [graɪnd]	3/1A schleifen
grinding ['graɪndɪŋ]	9/S knirschend
grip [grɪp]	5/1A Haftung
grit [grɪt]	5/1A Korn
guard plate ['gɑ:d ˌpleɪt]	1/3-HV Schutzblech

H

hacksaw ['hæksɔ:]	1/S Bügelsäge
hand brake ['hænbreɪk]	7/4A Handbremse
handling ['hændlɪŋ]	8/S Fahrverhalten
hang gliding ['hæŋ‿ˌglaɪdɪŋ]	12/4A Drachenfliegen
hatchback ['hætʃbæk]	3/S Steilheck
headlight ['hedlaɪt]	4/S Scheinwerfer
headliner ['hedlaɪnə]	10/1A Himmel
headrest ['hedrest]	8/S Kopfstütze
heavy-duty equipment [ˌhevɪdju:tɪ‿ɪ'kwɪpmənt]	12/1A Hochleistungsausrüstung
high-bay store ['haɪbeɪ ˌstɔ:]	10/1A Hochregallager
hip [hɪp]	8/3A Hüfte
hoist [hɔɪst]	10/4 Hebezug, Kettenzug
hole [həʊl]	1/1A Loch
hood [hʊd]	5/S (US) Motorhaube
hub [hʌb]	8/1E Nabe
hydraulic [haɪ'drɔ:lɪk]	8/2A hydraulisch

I

I put my foot in it. [aɪ ˌpʊt‿maɪ 'fʊt ɪn ɪt]	8/1B-HV Ich trete ins Fettnäpfchen.
i.e. (id est) [ˌaɪ'i:] [ɪd 'est]	6/1D d. h. (das heißt)
I'd like you to ... [aɪd‿'laɪk jʊ tʊ ...]	8/1B-HV Ich hätte gern, dass du/ihr ...
icy ['aɪsɪ]	9/3A-HV vereist, eisglatt
idle speed ['aɪdl ˌspi:d]	9/2 Leerlauf
ignite, v [ɪg'naɪt]	6/1B zünden
ignition [ɪg'nɪʃn]	6/1B Zündung
immersion bath [ɪ'mɜ:ʃn ˌbɑ:θ]	2/1B-HV Tauchbad
impact ['ɪmpækt]	8/3A Aufprall
improve, v [ɪm'pru:v]	3/1A verbessern
in charge of [ɪn 'tʃɑ:dʒ əv]	2/S verantwortlich für
include, v [ɪn'klu:d]	12/2B-HV enthalten
increase, v [ɪn'kri:s]	9/2 (Verkehr) zunehmen
indicator ['ɪndɪkeɪtə]	6/1B Blinker
induction stroke [ɪn'dʌkʃn ˌstrəʊk]	7/1 Ansaugtakt
injection nozzle [ɪn'dʒekʃn ˌnɒzl]	11/S Einspritzdüse
injection pump [ɪn'dʒekʃn ˌpʌmp]	7/S Einspritzpumpe
inlet (intake) valve ['ɪnlet ˌvælv] ['ɪnteɪk ˌvælv]	7/1A Einlassventil
insert, v [ɪn'sɜ:t]	8/1E hineinstecken
inspection [ɪn'spekʃn]	10/S Kontrolle, Prüfung
install, v [ɪn'stɔ:l]	2/S einbauen
instructor [ɪn'strʌktə]	1/3-HV Werkstattlehrer, Meister
insulated ['ɪnsjəleɪtɪd]	6/3 isoliert
intake manifold ['ɪnteɪk ˌmænɪfəʊld]	7/2A Einlasskrümmer
intake valve ['ɪnteɪk ˌvælv]	7/1A Einlassventil

internal combustion engine [ɪnˌtɜ:nl kəmˈbʌstʃn ˌendʒɪn]	7/1 Verbrennungsmotor
interval [ˈɪntəvl]	8/3A Zeitabstand
interview [ˈɪntəvju:]	12/1 Bewerbungsgespräch
invoice [ˈɪnvɔɪs]	11/1 Rechnung
involve, v [ɪnˈvɒlv]	1/S beinhalten

J

jack [dʒæk]	4/1A Wagenheber
jack stand [ˈdʒækˌstænd]	7/4C Unterstellbock
jig pallet [ˈdʒɪg ˌpælɪt]	3/1A Bauteilträger
job centre [ˈdʒɒb ˌsentə]	12/2A Arbeitsamt
join, v [dʒɔɪn]	4/S fügen, verbinden
joint [dʒɔɪnt]	9/3A-HV Gelenk

K

knowledge [ˈnɒlɪdʒ]	12/2C Wissen

L

label, v [ˈleɪbl]	9/2A beschriften
labour intensive [ˌleɪbər‿ɪnˈtensɪv]	10/1A arbeitsintensiv
layer [ˈleɪə]	5/1A Schicht
leak [li:k]	7/2A lecken, undicht sein; undichte Stelle
left-hand drive [ˌlefthænd‿ˈdraɪv]	9/2 Linkssteuerung
length [leŋθ]	1/2A Länge
level [ˈlevl]	5/1A Ebene, Niveau
liftgate [ˈlɪftgeɪt]	5/S (US) Heckklappe
limousine [ˌlɪməˈzi:n]	3/S Luxuslimousine
lock, v [lɒk]	9/2 sperren
locker-room [ˈlɒkəˌrʊm]	3/1A Umkleideraum
locking pliers [ˈlɒkɪŋ ˌplaɪəz]	5/1D Gripzange
Logistics [ləˈdʒɪstɪks]	2/S Logistik
look forward to, v [ˌlʊk ˈfɔ:wəd‿tʊ]	11/2A sich freuen auf
loosen, v [ˈlu:sn]	4/S lösen
lose*, v [lu:z]	6/1A verlieren
Ltd (limited) [ˌelti:ˈdi:] [ˈlɪmɪtɪd]	11/2A GmbH
lug wrench [ˈlʌg ˌrentʃ]	7/4C Kreuzschlüssel

M

machine tool [məˈʃi:n ˌtu:l]	1/S Werkzeugmaschine
mains [meɪnz]	6/1A Stromnetz-Hauptschalter
mains (electricity supply) [meɪnz elekˈtrɪsɪtɪ səˈplaɪ]	6/1A Stromnetz
mains tester [ˈmeɪnz ˌtestə]	6/S Phasenprüfer
maintain, v [meɪnˈteɪn]	3/1 instandhalten; erhalten
maintenance [ˈmeɪntənəns]	3/1A Instandhaltung
major [ˈmeɪdʒə]	3/1A größer
make* up, v [ˌmeɪk ˈʌp]	12/4B erfinden, sich aus denken
manual [ˈmænjʊəl]	11/S Handbuch
manufacture [ˌmænjəˈfæktʃə]	1/S Fertigung; fertigen; herstellen
manufacturer [ˌmænjəˈfæktʃərə]	1/1 Hersteller
mark, v [mɑ:k]	1/2A anreißen
marriage [ˈmærɪdʒ]	2/1B-HV Hochzeit
measure, v [ˈmeʒə]	1/3-HV messen
mechanical engineering [məˌkænɪkl endʒɪˈnɪərɪŋ]	1/S Maschinenbau
mediate, v [ˈmi:dɪeɪt]	10/3 (Inhalte) vermitteln
meet* demands [ˌmi:t‿dɪˈmɑ:ndz]	3/S Anforderungen erfüllen
member [ˈmembə]	3/1A Träger
memo [ˈmeməʊ]	6/1C Kurznachricht
mention, v [ˈmenʃn]	2/1D erwähnen
message [ˈmesɪdʒ]	6/1C-HV Nachricht
metal panel [ˌmetl ˈpænl]	3/1A Beplankung
minimize, v [ˈmɪnɪmaɪz]	8/S minimieren
misfire, v [mɪsˈfaɪə]	7/2A zünden mit Zündaussetzern
monitor, v [ˈmɒnɪtə]	8/3A überwachen
most recent [məʊst ˈri:sənt]	12/2B-HV neuester, letzter
MOT (Ministry of Transport) [ˌmɪnɪstrɪ‿əvˈtrænspɔ:t]	10/2 TÜV (Technischer Überwachungsverein)
motive power [ˌməʊtɪv ˈpaʊə]	7/1 Schub(-kraft)
mould, v [məʊld]	8/3A formen
mount, v [maʊnt]	4/1A montieren
mountings [ˈmaʊntɪŋz]	10/2-HV Aufhängung
multimeter [ˈmʌltɪˌmi:tə]	6/S Vielfachmessgerät für Volt und Ampere
multi-purpose [ˌmʌltɪˈpɜ:pəs]	3/S Mehrzweck-

N

negotiable: The salary is negotiable. [nɪˈgəʊʃɪəbl] [ðə ˈsælərɪ‿ɪz nɪˌgəʊʃɪəbl]	12/1A verhandelbar: Über das Gehalt kann verhandelt werden.
niche [ni:ʃ]	3/S Nische
nip off, v [ˌnɪp ˈɒf]	6/S abzwicken
nowadays [ˈnaʊədeɪz]	9/2 heutzutage
nut [nʌt]	4/S Mutter

O

obstruct, v [əbˈstrʌkt]	10/5 versperren
occasional(ly) [əˈkeɪʒənl] [əˈkeɪʒənlɪ]	5/1A gelegentlich
occupant [ˈɒkjəpənt]	8/S Insasse, Insassin
octagonal [ɒkˈtægənl]	1/1A achteckig
offer, v [ˈɒfə]	8/1 anbieten

off-road vehicle [ˌɒfrəʊd ˈvɪəkl] 9/3A-HV Geländefahrzeug
oil dipstick [ˈɔɪl ˌdɪpstɪk] 7/S Ölmessstab, -peilstab
oil pan [ˈɔɪl ˌpæn] 7/S Ölwanne
oil-drain screw [ˈɔɪlˌdreɪn ˌskru:] 7/S Ölablassschraube
operation [ˌɒpəˈreɪʃn] 7/4A Arbeitsweise
outlet valve [ˈaʊtlet ˌvælv] 7/1A Auslassventil
outsell*, v [ˌaʊtˈsel] 3/S mehr als … verkaufen
oxygen [ˈɒksɪdʒən] 4/S Sauerstoff

P

Paint Shop [ˈpeɪnt ˌʃɒp] 2/S Lackiererei
parking lock [ˈpɑ:kɪŋ ˌlɒk] 9/2 Parksperre
pay [peɪ] 12/1A Lohn
pedestrian [pəˈdestrɪən] 8/3A Fußgänger/in
permanent(ly) [ˈpɜ:mənənt] [ˈpɜ:mənəntlɪ] 6/1A ständig, regelmäßig
pincers [ˈpɪnsəz] 6/S Kneifzange
pipe [paɪp] 4/1A Rohr
pipe bracket [ˈpaɪp‿ˌbrækɪt] 4/1A Rohrschelle
piston ring [ˈpɪstən ˌrɪŋ] 7/S Kolbenring
plant [plɑ:nt] 2/1A Fabrik
plaster [ˈplɑ:stə] 4/4-HV Pflaster
plastics [ˈplæstɪks] 4/S Plastik
plate [pleɪt] 1/2A Platte
pliers [ˈplaɪəz] 1/S Zange
power stroke [ˈpaʊə ˌstrəʊk] 7/1 Arbeitstakt
power tool [ˈpaʊə ˌtu:l] 1/S Elektrowerkzeug
power windows [ˈpaʊə ˌwɪndəʊz] 6/S elektrische Fensterheber
practically-minded [ˌpræktɪkəlɪ ˈmaɪndɪd] 12/1A praktisch denkend
prefer, v [prɪˈfɜ:] 9/2 bevorzugen
Press Shop [ˈpres‿ˌʃɒp] 2/S Presswerk
prevent, v [prɪˈvent] 5/1A verhindern
preventive [prɪˈventətɪv] 8/3A vorbeugend
primary school [ˈpraɪmərɪ sku:l] 12/2B-HV Grundschule
primer [ˈpraɪmə] 5/1A Grundierung
production fitter [prəˈdʌkʃn ˌfɪtə] 3/1 Fertigungsmechaniker/in
progressively [prəˈgresɪvlɪ] 5/1A stufenweise
protection [prəˈtekʃn] 1/1A Schutz
protective clothes [prəˌtektɪv ˈkləʊðz] 2/1B-HV Schutzkleidung
provide, v [prəˈvaɪd] 5/1A sorgen für; versorgen
put* through, v [ˌpʊt ˈθru:] 6/1C (Telefon) verbinden

Q

quality assurance [ˈkwɒlətɪ‿əˌʃɔ:rəns] 12/2C Qualitätssicherung

R

radiator [ˈreɪdɪeɪtə] 6/1B Kühler
radiator fan [ˈreɪdɪeɪtə ˌfæn] 7/S Kühlerventilator, -lüfter
rag [ræg] 1/3-HV Lappen
raise, v [reɪz] 7/4A anheben
rapid(ly) [ˈræpɪd] [ˈræpɪdlɪ] 9/2 schnell, rasch
ratchet [ˈrætʃɪt] 4/2B Rätsche
reach, v [ri:tʃ] 9/S erreichen
rear [ˈrɪə] 4/S hintere, Rück-
rear shelf panel [ˈrɪəʃelf ˌpænl] 5/S Heckablageblech
rear-wheel drive [ˌrɪəwi:l ˈdraɪv] 9/3A-HV Hinterradantrieb
reception [rɪˈsepʃn] 1/1 Empfang
reduce, v [rɪˈdju:s] 10/3 verringern, reduzieren
referee [ˌrefəˈri:] 12/3 Person, die als Referenz dient
release [rɪˈli:s] 9/1 lösen, loslassen; Entriegelung
relieve, v [rɪˈli:v] 9/2 befreien, entlasten
remind, v: That reminds me of … [rɪˈmaɪnd] [ˌðæt rɪˈmaɪndz mɪ‿əv] 6/1A erinnern: Das erinnert mich an …
remote(-controlled) [rɪˌməʊt kənˈtrəʊld] 10/S ferngesteuert
remove, v [rɪˈmu:v] 5/1A entfernen
replace, v [rɪˈpleɪs] 3/1A ersetzen
request, v [rɪˈkwest] 8/1 bitten
require, v [rɪˈkwaɪə] 4/S erfordern
required [rɪˈkwaɪəd] 11/S erforderlich, verlangt
researcher [rɪˈsɜ:tʃə] 8/3A Forscher/in
responsibility [rɪˌspɒnsəˈbɪlətɪ] 2/2A Verantwortung, Verantwortlichkeit
restrain, v [rɪˈstreɪn] 8/3A zurückhalten
restricted area [rɪˌstrɪktɪd ˈeərɪə] 2/1B-HV Sperrzone
résumé [ˈrezju:meɪ] 12/2A (US) Lebenslauf
retaining bolt [rɪˈteɪnɪŋ ˌbəʊlt] 8/1E Befestigungsbolzen, -schraube
reverse gear [rɪˌvɜ:s ˈgɪə] 9/2 Rückwärtsgang
ribbed V-belt [ˌrɪbd ˈvi:belt] 7/S Keilrippenriemen
rigger's gloves [ˈrɪgəz ˌglʌvz] 2/4B Arbeitshandschuhe
right angle [ˈraɪtˌæŋgl] 1/2A rechter Winkel
ring* back, v [ˌrɪŋ ˈbæk] 11/S zurückrufen
ring spanner [ˈrɪŋ ˌspænə] 4/2B Ringschlüssel
rinse, v [rɪns] 5/1A spülen
rivet welding [ˈrɪvɪt ˌweldɪŋ] 3/1A Nietschweißen
riveting [ˈrɪvɪtɪŋ] 10/4 Vernieten, Nietentechnik
road conditions [ˈrəʊd kənˌdɪʃnz] 9/3A-HV Straßenverhältnisse
roof panel [ˈru:f ˌpænl] 5/S Dachblech
rough [rʌf] 3/1A rau
roughing file [ˈrʌfɪŋ ˌfaɪl] 1/2A Schruppfeile
round nose pliers [ˌraʊnd nəʊz ˈplaɪəz] 6/S Flachrundzange
rubber [ˈrʌbə] 10/1A Gummi
run* out of [ˌrʌn ˈaʊt əv] 4/4-HV kein … mehr haben

rust [rʌst]	8/1B-HV Rost
rusty ['rʌstɪ]	4/1A rostig, verrostet

S

safety ['seɪftɪ]	1/5 Sicherheit
salary ['sælərɪ]	12/1A Gehalt
salary requirement ['sælərɪ rɪˌkwaɪəmənt]	12/3 Gehaltsvorstellung
saloon [sə'lu:n]	3/S Limousine
sand, v [sænd]	5/1A schleifen
sanding drill ['sændɪŋ ˌdrɪl]	5/1A Elektroschleifer
score, v [skɔ:]	5/1A kratzen
scrap [skræp]	4/2A Schrott
scratch, v [skrætʃ]	1/3-HV (ver-)kratzen
screw [skru:]	4/S Schraube; schrauben
screwdriver ['skru:ˌdraɪvə]	1/S Schraubendreher
screwdriver (cross head) [ˌkrɒshed 'skru:ˌdraɪvə]	6/S Kreuzschlitzschraubendreher
screwdriver (slotted) [ˌslɒtɪd 'skru:ˌdraɪvə]	6/S Schlitzschraubendreher
scriber ['skraɪbə]	1/2A Anreißnadel
seat belt ['si:t ˌbelt]	8/S Sitzgurt
seat pan ['si:t ˌpæn]	10/4 Sitzwanne, -schale
section steel ['sekʃn ˌsti:l]	1/3-HV U-Stahl
sedan ['sɪ:dæn]	3/S (US) Limousine
selector lever [sə'lektə ˌli:və]	9/2 Wählhebel
self-tapping screw [ˌself'tæpɪŋ ˌskru:]	5/1D Blechschraube
service / servicing ['sɜ:vɪs] ['sɜ:vɪsɪŋ]	11/S Kundendienst
shape [ʃeɪp]	5/1A Form
sheet metal [ˌʃi:t 'metl]	2/1B-HV Stahlblech; Pressteil
shield [ʃi:ld]	8/3A Schutzschild
shift [ʃɪft]	3/1A Schicht
shift, v [ʃɪft]	9/1 bewegen
Shipping ['ʃɪpɪŋ]	2/S Versand
shop floor [ˌʃɒp 'flɔ:]	1/1 Werkstattetage
side aperture panel [ˌsaɪd 'æpətʃə ˌpænl]	5/S Seitenblech
side (curtain) airbag ['saɪd kɜ:tən 'eəbæg] ['saɪd 'eəbæg]	8/3A Seitenairbag
side panel ['saɪd ˌpænl]	2/1B-HV Seitenblech
silencer pads ['saɪlənsə ˌpædz]	10/1A schalldämpfende Füllung
similar ['sɪmɪlə]	8/1B ähnlich
skid [skɪd]	10/1A Förderschlitten
skid, v [skɪd]	9/3A-HV schleudern
slack [slæk]	8/S schlaff
slippery ['slɪpərɪ]	8/S rutschig
smooth [smu:ð]	5/1A glatt; eben
smoothness ['smu:ðnəs]	3/1A Ebenheit
socket ['sɒkɪt]	4/2B Steckeinsatz
soft-face hammer [ˌsɒftfeɪs 'hæmə]	5/1A Aluhammer
spanner ['spænə]	1/S Schraubenschlüssel

spare [speə]	6/1A Ersatz-
spare part [ˌspeə 'pɑ:t]	4/1A Ersatzteil
Spare Parts Store [ˌspeə 'pɑ:ts‿ˌstɔ:]	4/1A Ersatzteillager
spark [spɑ:k]	2/1B-HV Funke
spark plug ['spɑ:kplʌg]	7/S Zündkerze
specified ['spesɪfaɪd]	8/1E vorgegeben
sport utility vehicle (SUV) [ˌspɔ:t ju:'tɪlətɪ ˌvɪəkl]	3/S Geländewagen
spot welding ['spɒt ˌweldɪŋ]	3/1A Punktschweißen
square [skweə]	1/S Winkel
stall, v [stɔ:l]	9/1 (Motor) abwürgen
stamp, v [stæmp]	2/S pressen
starter motor ['stɑ:tə ˌməʊtə]	6/1A Starter
starter pinion gear ['stɑ:tə ˌpɪnjən ˌgɪə]	7/S Anlasserritzel
starve, v [stɑ:v]	8/1B-HV verhungern
station wagon ['steɪʃn ˌwægən]	3/S (US) Kombiwagen
stay alive, v [ˌsteɪ‿ə'laɪv]	8/S am Leben bleiben
steel [sti:l]	4/S Stahl
steering column ['stɪərɪŋ ˌkɒləm]	10/S Lenksäule
steering wheel ['stɪərɪŋ ˌwi:l]	8/S Lenkrad
stock [stɒk]	10/3 (Material-) Bestand
straighten out, v [ˌstreɪtn 'aʊt]	5/1D ausbeulen
strength [streŋkθ]	12/3 Stärke
stretch, v [stretʃ]	5/1A ausdehnen
strip, v [strɪp]	6/2 abisolieren
stroke [strəʊk]	7/1 Takt, Hub
stud welding ['stʌd ˌweldɪŋ]	3/1A Bolzenschweißen
sub-assembly ['sʌbəˌsemblɪ]	3/1A Baugruppe
succeed, v [sək'si:d]	9/1 Erfolg haben
suck, v [ˌsʌk]	7/1A (an)saugen
suggest, v [sə'dʒest]	8/1 vorschlagen
suggestion [sə'dʒestʃn]	8/1A Vorschlag
suitable [su:təbl]	4/S passend
sunroof aperture panel [ˌsʌnru:f 'æpətʃə ˌpænl]	5/S Schiebedach-Rahmenblech
sunshade ['sʌnʃeɪd]	10/S Sonnenblende
supervision [ˌsu:pə'vɪʒn]	8/1B Aufsicht
supervisor ['su:pəˌvaɪzə]	10/3 Aufseher/in, Aufsicht
supplier [sə'plaɪə]	12/2C Lieferant
supply, v [sə'plaɪ]	2/S liefern; versorgen
support service [sə'pɔ:t ˌsɜ:vɪs]	11/2A Kundenbetreuung
support, v [se'pɔ:t]	7/4A (ab-)stützen
surface ['sɜ:fɪs]	1/3-HV Oberfläche
surprise, v [sə'praɪz]	11/1 überraschen
surroundings [sə'raʊndɪŋz]	8/3A Umgebung
suspension [sə'spenʃn]	10/1A Aufhängung
synchronized ['sɪŋkrənaɪzd]	9/S synchronisiert

T

tack-weld, v ['tæk,weld] 3/1A heftschweißen
tail panel ['teɪl ,pænl] 5/S Heck(abschluss)blech
Take your time! [,teɪk jɔ: 'taɪm] 8/1B-HV Lass dir Zeit!
tapescript ['teɪpskrɪpt] 2/1E Hörverstehenstext
tense, v [tens] 8/3A (sich) straffen
tighten, v ['taɪtn] 4/S (fest) anziehen
tilt, v [tɪlt] 8/3A kippen
tinted ['tɪntɪd] 10/S (Glas) getönt
tip [tɪp] 1/1A Spitze
tool [tu:l] 1/S Werkzeug
top dead centre (TDC) [,tɒp ,ded 'sentə] [,ti:di:'si:] 7/1 oberer Totpunkt
torque [tɔ:k] 8/1E Dreh-, Anzugsmoment
torque converter ['tɔ:k‿kən,vɜ:tə] 9/2 Drehmomentwandler
torque wrench ['tɔ:k rentʃ] 4/3 Drehmomentschlüssel
tow, v [təʊ] 9/2 (Auto) abschleppen
toxic ['tɒksɪk] 1/5 giftig
traction control (TC) ['trækʃn kən,trəʊl] [,ti:'si:] 8/S Antriebsschlupfregelung
trainee [,treɪ'ni:] 1/S Auszubildende/r
transmission [trænz'mɪʃn] 9/S Getriebe
tray [treɪ] 4/2A Tablett
treat, v [tri:t] 2/S behandeln
trim [trɪm] 10/1A Innenausstattung
tune-up [,tju:n 'ʌp] 12/1A (Motor) Tuning
twist drill ['twɪst‿drɪl] 1/2A Spiralbohrer
tyre ['taɪə] 8/S Reifen

U

underbody ['ʌndəbɒdɪ] 3/1A Unterboden
uninjured [ʌn'ɪndʒəd] 8/S unverletzt
unnecessary [ʌn'nesəsərɪ] 10/S unnötig
unscrew, v [ʌn'skru:] 4/2A abschrauben
unusual [ʌn'ju:ʒʊəl] 11/2A ungewöhnlich
urgent(ly) ['ɜ:dʒənt] ['ɜ:dʒəntlɪ] 6/1C-HV dringend

V

vacancy ['veɪkənsɪ] 12/1 freie Stelle
valve spring ['vælv ,sprɪŋ] 7/S Ventilfeder
various ['veərɪəs] 9/3 verschiedenartig
V-belt ['vi:,belt] 6/1A Keilriemen
vertical slide [,vɜ:tɪkl 'slaɪd] 1/1A Senkrechtschlitten
vice [vaɪs] 1/S Schraubstock
vice jaw ['vaɪs ,dʒɔ:] 1/3-HV Schraubstockbacken, Spannbacken
vocational school [vəʊ'keɪʃənl ,sku:l] 3/3A Berufsschule
voltage ['vəʊltɪdʒ] 1/5 Spannung

W

waste [weɪst] 10/S Verschwendung; Abfall
wear and tear [,weər‿ənd‿'teə] 9/3A-HV Verschleiß, Abnutzung
wear out, v [,weər‿'aʊt] 9/3A-HV (sich abnutzen)
weigh, v [weɪ] 2/1B-HV wiegen
weld, v [weld] 2/S schweißen
welding gun ['weldɪŋ‿gʌn] 2/1B-HV Schweißpistole
welding torch ['weldɪŋ ,tɔ:tʃ] 4/S Schweißbrenner
wheel house ['wi:lhaʊs] 5/S Radlauf
wheel rim ['wi:lrɪm] 7/4A Felge
whiplash ['wɪplæʃ] 8/S Schleudertrauma
width [wɪtθ] 1/2A Breite
windscreen ['wɪnskri:n] 8/S Windschutzscheibe
wing [wɪŋ] 4/2 Kotflügel
wing apron ['wɪŋ ,eɪprən] 4/2 Motorraumseitenteil
wire brush [,waɪə 'brʌʃ] 5/1A Stahlbürste
wire stripper ['waɪə ,strɪpə] 6/S Abisolierzange
wire stripping pliers ['waɪə ,strɪpɪŋ ,plaɪəz] 6/S Abisolierzange
wiring ['waɪərɪŋ] 2/1B-HV Leitungen
wiring harness ['waɪərɪŋ ,hɑ:nɪs] 6/1B Kabelbaum
wobble ['wɒbl] 7/4 Wackeln; wackeln
word processing program ['wɜ:d ,prəʊsesɪŋ 'prəʊgræm] 12/3 Textverarbeitungsprogramm
workbench ['wɜ:kbentʃ] 1/1A Werkbank
workshop ['wɜ:kʃɒp] 1/S Werkstatt
worn to excess [,wɔ:n tʊ‿ɪk'ses] 10/2-HV vollständig abgenutzt
Would you like me to ...? [,wʊd‿jʊ 'laɪk mɪ tʊ ...] 8/1B-HV Möchtest du, dass ich ...?
wrap, v [ræp] 5/1A einwickeln
wrench [rentʃ] 4/3 Schraubenschlüssel

Hörverstehenstexte

Die hier nicht aufgeführten Texte der Kassette/CD sind bereits im vorderen Teil des Buches in den Units abgedruckt.

Unit 1

3A+B

Christian: Hi, Sarah, what are you doing there? You look rather busy.
Sarah: Hi, Christian. I've got to prepare my workbench for finishing this section steel. Do you know where I can find the right file?
Christian: Yes, it's in the drawer under your bench plate, you see, next to the hammer.
Sarah: OK, here it is. What else do I need? – Oh, yes, there's the square to measure the right angles and the edges of the section steel.
Christian: And don't forget the guard plates.
Sarah: What do I need them for?
Christian: Well, when you clamp the section steel into the vice, you have to protect the sides of the steel, so you put the guard plates between the steel and the vice jaws.
Sarah: Oh, I see. So I won't scratch the surface of the section steel that I have to finish.
Christian: Now you've got it. And put all the tools on a rag on your bench plate next to the vice.
Sarah: Yeah, sure. So Herr Berger, our instructor, will be happy, too.

Unit 2

1B

Christian: At the Press Shop, of course … where the sheet metal is brought in for stamping. They're responsible for manufacturing the metal body parts. Have you ever seen the enormous dies in the presses?
Sarah: Not in real life, only in pictures.
Christian: They must weigh tons. Just wait till you see those side panels coming out of the presses. By the way, it's very loud in there so you'll need some ear protection. When the parts are pressed they are transported to the Body Shop and then they're welded together to form the body. Nowadays robots do almost all the welding.
Mike: Wow, I'm looking forward to seeing them in action.
Christian: Don't forget to wear your safety glasses. There might be sparks flying from the welding guns. Our instructor told me that we aren't going to go to the Paint Shop on Monday. You know, the bodies are dipped into a huge immersion bath. It's a restricted area and we'll have to get special permission and protective clothes.
Sarah: Are we going to get a chance to see the Final Assembly, too?
Christian: Yeah. We're going to see them installing the electrical wiring … and the marriage of the chassis and the body. That's brilliant! It's amazing how they get it spot on each time.

Unit 4

4

Elaine: Hello?
John: Hi, this is John.
Elaine: Oh hello, John, how are you?
John: Fine, thanks. Err ..., could you help me?
Elaine: Of course, what's the problem?
John: One of my trainees has cut his hand on a sharp edge.
Elaine: Was he wearing his gloves?
John: No, he forgot to put them on. Now I need a plaster.
Elaine: Have you checked your first aid kit? You know, each workshop has got one.
John: Yes, I know. I've checked mine, but we've run out of plasters.
Elaine: All right, John. Why don't you send one of your trainees over, and I'll give him some.
John: That's very kind of you, Elaine. Thanks.
Elaine: You're welcome, John. Bye.
John: Bye.

Unit 6

1C

Sarah: CarFit, Spare Parts Store, Sarah Jackson speaking.
Bill Wall: Hello, this is Bill Wall from Automobile Spare Parts in Cork. Could I speak to Steffen Berger, please?
Sarah: Oh, I'm sorry, but Herr Berger isn't in at the moment, and he won't be back before tomorrow afternoon, I'm afraid. Would you like to leave a message for him?
Bill Wall: I see, well, if you'd be so kind and tell him that we urgently need a new generator for the TR 1992 model. The part number is TR 1243 B9203. And we would appreciate a circuit diagram as well, because we've lost ours, I'm afraid.
Sarah: OK, I've got that. Just to repeat that: the part number is TR 1243 B2903 ...
Bill Wall: No, no, no, no, it's 9203 ...
Sarah: Oh yes, 9203, plus a circuit diagram. Has Herr Berger got your address?
Bill Wall: Yes, I'm sure he has.
Sarah: OK, if that's all, I'll give him this message as soon as possible.
Bill Wall: That's very kind of you. Thanks and goodbye.
Sarah: Bye.

Unit 7

3

Sarah: What did you do yesterday, Mike? Did you go to the Sports Club?
Mike: Yes. I went there with Christian.
Sarah: Did you play tennis?
Mike: Yes, we did.

Sarah: Christian is great, isn't he? Did he win the match?
Mike: Yes, he won easily.
Sarah: What did you do in the evening?
Mike: I stayed at home and watched television. What did you do?
Sarah: I went to a rock concert. The TOP DEAD CENTRES. They were just brilliant.
Mike: They played techno I suppose.
Sarah: No, mechano, actually!!

Unit 8

1B+C

S. Berger: Before you start removing the brake I'd like you to put on your filtering masks. There might be some hazardous dust in the system.
Sarah: Sure. Hey, Mike yours seems to be damaged, would you like me to get you a new one?
Mike: Thanks, Sarah, that's very kind of you but I can manage with this one. Is it all right if we start now, Herr Berger? We're short of time.
S. Berger: Yes, go ahead.
Sarah: Mike, can you see those two bolts securing the brake caliper bracket? Well, do you think you could remove them while I'm taking off the brake pad sensor?
Mike: Certainly, but we've got to be careful not to let the caliper hang on the brake pipe. Shall I slip it off the disc?
Sarah: Thanks. Herr Berger? May I take a look at it this time?
S. Berger: That's fine with me. Watch out for the scoring. Why don't you check the disc thickness?
Sarah: Right. Where's the micrometer? Mike, can you get it for me, please?
Mike: Yeah, all right, take your time, will you? Can I check the disc for rust now?
S. Berger: I'm afraid not. You'll have to do it after the break. Could you tidy up the tools? It's time to go to lunch.
Sarah: I'm sorry we can't, Herr Berger. We're starving and we haven't got any energy left.
S. Berger: What?
Sarah: I was only joking, really. How about going to the canteen now, Mike, before I put my foot in it again?
Mike: Yes, let's go, shall we?

Unit 9

3 A+B

Sarah: You know, back home in the States, there are a lot of four-wheel drive cars, especially on farms, where you need off-road vehicles.
Mike: Yeah, I just love them. They look cool, and they are much better than rear-wheel drive cars.

Christian: But you don't need an off-road car here in Germany, unless you have to drive on a lot of dirt roads like in forests.

Sarah: Yeah, you're right.

Mike: All right, but we also have slippery roads, especially in winter, when the roads are icy. The automatic four-wheel drive is a great help, because it comes on automatically when you need it.

Christian: Yes, and that's a good safety feature as well. But we don't have such road conditions very often. I guess a front-wheel drive is good enough.

Sarah: Yes, I agree. And in the States, even all the smaller cars have had front-wheel drive for years now. They are safer because they don't skid when you speed up.

Mike: But the drive shafts wear out faster because of the stress on the joints. And that's the reason why heavy cars with front engines must have rear-wheel drive …

Sarah: … and: the steering is also easier with a rear-wheel drive.

Christian: Yeah, true, but don't forget that four-wheel drive cars consume more petrol and there's more wear and tear.

Unit 10

2

Good afternoon, everybody.

Well, as you all know, the braking system is probably the most important feature in the car because it can prevent accidents and loss of life or serious injury. That's why we check it very carefully. I can't possibly mention all the checks done because we'll have to talk about the steering and the transmission, too.

Now, we divide the inspection up into four main areas:

the footbrake, the handbrake or reserve brake as it is sometimes called, under the bonnet and finally under the vehicle itself.

When checking the footbrake we make sure that the pedal rubber is not worn too much and that the mountings are not corroded. Our people are trained to see exactly what degree of wear and tear is allowed.

We also check to see if the metal and flexible pipes are corroded or maybe even broken or leaking.

It all depends on how well we can see them but we also inspect the brake pads to see if they are in good condition. A lot of this is still done manually especially for the mechanical parts.

We test the actual braking performance using roller test equipment; this is measured electronically and not just left to human judgement.

Oh, I forgot to mention that we also turn the engine on and apply the brakes to check the master cylinder and the servo for leaks.

Unit 12

2B

Christian: Sarah, what do you think I should do first when I'm writing an application in English?

Sarah: Well, first I would write the opening address like "Dear Sirs" or "Dear Sir or Madam". Then I would go on with the job you would like to apply for.

Christian: And what about my career? Do I start with my education and carry on with my training?

Sarah: If you apply to a company in the USA or in Great Britain, you will have to start with the most recent job.

Christian: That's different in Germany. If you were interested in a job here, you would start with your education at primary school.

Sarah: Yes, I know. And it's the same with the CV. If you wrote the CV for an application in America you would first write about the most recent experience and after that about your training or education.

Christian: OK, that's clear now. Could you give me any tips about the CV?

Sarah: Well, let's see. The CV shouldn't be longer than one or two pages. And, you should use good quality paper, of course.

Christian: What about a photo?

Sarah: You don't have to include a photo. But if you had any references, you could include the addresses of the referees as well.

Christian: Would you say anything about the salary?

Sarah: No, I wouldn't if you were not asked to do so. … And don't forget to keep a copy of your own CV, because if you are invited for an interview, you should look at it again.

Christian: Well, thanks a lot, Sarah.

Fachwortschatz deutsch-englisch

(Weitere Fachbegriffe befinden sich im Lehrerhandbuch.)

A

abbauen – demount, v
abisolieren – strip, v
Abisolierzange – wire stripper
abklemmen – disconnect, v
abmontieren – demount, v
abnutzen (sich) – wear out, v
abschleppen (Auto) – tow, v
abschrauben – unscrew, v
abstützen – support, v
Abteilung – department
abwürgen (Motor) – stall, v
abzwicken – nip off, v
Achsantrieb – axle drive
achteckig – octagonal
Aluhammer – soft-face hammer
Anlasserritzel – starter pinion gear
anreißen – mark, v
Anreißnadel – scriber
(an)saugen – suck (in), v
Antiblockiersystem – anti-lock braking system (ABS)
Antriebsschlupfregelung – traction control (TC)
Antriebswelle – drive shaft
anziehen – tighten, v
Arbeitshandschuhe – rigger's gloves
Arbeitsweise – operation
Armaturenbrett – dashboard
A-Säule – A-pillar
Aufbaustation – framing station
Aufhängung – mountings
aufladen (Batterie) – charge, v
aufnehmen – absorb, v
Aufprall – impact
Aufseher/in – supervisor
auftragen – apply, v
ausbeulen – straighten out, v
ausdehnen – expand, stretch, v
auseinander nehmen – disassemble, v
ausgestattet sein – be equipped
Auslassventil – outlet valve
Auspuff – exhaust
Auspuffkrümmer – exhaust manifold
Ausrüstung – gear, kit
Ausstattung – equipment
Ausstoßtakt – exhaust stroke
Auszubildende/r – trainee
Autowerkstatt – garage

B

Bankschraubstock – bench vice
Batterie – battery
Baugruppe – sub-assembly
Bauteilträger – jig pallet
Befestigungsbolzen, -schraube – retaining bolt
befördern – convey, v
Beplankung – metal panel, cladding
Beschichtung – coat
Beule – dent
Blechschraube – self-tapping screw
Blinker – indicator
Bodenbelag – carpeting
bohren; Bohrer – drill
Bohrfutter – drill chuck
Bolzen, Schraube – bolt
Bolzenschweißen – stud welding
Bremsbelag – brake pad
bremsen; Bremse – brake
Bremsleitung – brake pipe
B-Säulen-Verstärkung – B-pillar reinforcement
Bügelsäge, Eisensäge – hacksaw

C

Chassis – chassis

D

Dachblech – roof panel
Dichtmanschette – gasket
Dreh-, Anzugsmoment – torque
Drehmomentwandler – torque converter
Durchmesser – diameter

E

einbauen – install, v
Einlasskrümmer – intake manifold
Einlassventil – intake valve, inlet valve
Einrichtung – facility
einspannen – clamp, v
Einspritzdüse – injection nozzle
Einspritzpumpe – injection pump
einstellen; (Gang) einlegen – engage, v
elektrische Fensterheber – power windows
elektrischer Strom – current
Elektroschleifer – sanding drill
Elektrowerkzeug – power tool
Endmontage – Final Assembly
entgraten – debur, v
Entriegelung – release
entsorgen – dispose of, v
entwickeln – develop, v
Entwicklung – development
Ersatzteil – spare part
Ersatzteillager – spare parts store
erzeugen (Energie) – generate, v
ESP – electronic stability control (program) (ESP)

F

Fabrik – plant, factory
Fahrgestell – chassis
Fahrverhalten – handling
fehlzünden – backfire, v
feilen; Feile – file
Felge – wheel rim
ferngesteuert – remote-controlled
Fernsteuerung – remote control
fertigen; Fertigung – manufacture
Fertigungsmechaniker/in – production fitter
Fett, Schmiere – grease
Feuerlöscher – fire extinguisher
Flachmeißel – cold chisel
Flachrundzange – round nose pliers
Flüssigkeit – fluid
Förderer – conveyor
Förderschlitten – skid
Form – shape
formen – mould, v
Frontantrieb – front-wheel drive
fügen – join, v
Führerschein – driving licence, (US) driver's license
Fünfgangschaltgetriebe – 5-speed manual transmission
Funke – spark

G

Gang (Schaltung) – gear
Gaspedal – acceleration pedal
gegen Diebstahl – anti-theft
Geländefahrzeug – off-road vehicle
Geländewagen – sport utility vehicle (SUV)
Gelenk – joint
Geschwindikeitsregler – cruise control
getönt (Glas) – tinted
Getriebe – transmission
Gleichstrom – direct current (DC)
Gripzange – locking pliers
Grundierung – primer
Gummi – rubber
Gurtstraffer – belt pre-tensioner

H

Haftung – grip
Halter – bracket
Handbremse – hand brake
Handbuch – manual
Händler – dealer
Hebebühne – car lift
Hebezug – hoist
Heckablageblech – rear shelf panel
Heckantrieb – rear-wheel drive
Heck(abschluss)blech – tail panel
Heckklappe – (US) liftgate
heftschweißen – tack-weld, v
Heftstation – framing station
herstellen – manufacture, v
Hersteller – manufacturer
Himmel – headliner
Hinterradantrieb – rear-wheel drive
Hochleistungsausrüstung – heavy-duty equipment
Hochregallager – high-bay store
Hochzeit (Zusammenbau) – marriage
Hub – stroke

I

Imbusschraube – Allen-head screw
Innenausstattung – trim
Innensechskantschraube – Allen-head screw
Insasse, Insassin – occupant
instandhalten – maintain, v
Instandhaltung – maintenance
Instrumententräger – dashboard support
isoliert (Kabel) – insulated

K

Kabelbaum – wiring harness
Kante – edge
Karosserieteil – body part
kegelsenken – countersink, v
Keilriemen – V-belt
Keilrippenriemen – ribbed V-belt
Kettenzug – hoist
Kfz- – automotive
kleben – bond, v
Kleben – bonding
Klebstoff – adhesive
knallen (bei Fehlzündung) – backfire, v
Kneifzange – pincers
Kolbenring – piston ring
Kombiwagen – estate car, (US) station wagon
Kombizange – combination pliers
konstruieren – design, v
Kontrolle – inspection
Korn – grit
körnen – centre punch, v
Kotflügel – wing, (US) fender
Kraftbegrenzer – force limiter
Kraftstoff – fuel
Kraftstoffleitung – fuel line
Kraftstoffverbrauch – fuel consumption
Kraftübertragung – drive train, (US) power train
kratzen – score, v
Kreuzschlitzschraubendreher – crosshead screwdriver
Kreuzschlüssel – lug wrench
Kühler – radiator
Kühlerventilator, -lüfter – radiator fan
Kundendienst – service, servicing
Kupplung – clutch
Kurbelwelle – crankshaft

L

Lackiererei – Paint Shop
Laderoboter - handling robot
Lager (technisch) – bearing
Lappen – rag
Leerlauf – idle speed
Lehrling – apprentice
Leiter (elektrisch) – conductor
Leitungen – wiring
Lenkrad – steering wheel
Lenksäule – steering column
Lichtmaschine – generator
Lieferant – supplier
Limousine – saloon, (US) sedan
Linkssteuerung – left-hand drive
Loch – hole
Logistik – Logistics
lösen – loosen, release, v
loslassen – release, v
Luxuslimousine – limousine

M

Marke – brand
Maschinenbau – mechanical engineering
Mechaniker/in – mechanic
Mehrzweck- – multi-purpose
Meister – instructor
messen – measure, v
Montage – assembly
montieren – mount, v
Motor – engine
Motorhaube – bonnet, (US) hood
Motorpanne, -schaden – engine breakdown
Motorraumseitenteil – wing apron
Motorraum – engine compartment
Mutter – nut

N

Nabe – hub
Nietentechnik – riveting
Nietschweißen – rivet welding
Niveau – level
Nockenwelle – camshaft

O

oberer Totpunkt – top dead centre (TDC)
Oberfläche – surface
Ölablassschraube – oil-drain screw
Ölfilter – oil filter
Ölmessstab, -peilstab – oil dipstick
Ölwanne – oil pan

P

Parksperre – parking lock
Pegel – level
Phasenprüfer – mains tester
Planetengetriebe – downstream planetary gearset
Plastik – plastics
Platte – plate
Pleuel(-stange) – connecting rod
pressen – stamp, v
Press-Stempel, -Werkzeug – die (press)
Presswerk – Press Shop
Prüfung – inspection
Punktschweißen – spot welding

Q

Qualitätssicherung – quality assurance
Querträger – cross member
Querträger unter Windlauf – A-pillar cross member, (US) cowl cross member

R

Radlauf – wheel house
Rätsche – ratchet
rechter Winkel – right angle
Ringschlüssel – ring spanner
Rohbau (Fertigung) – Body Shop
Rohbaukarrosse – body shell
Rohr – pipe
Rohrschelle – pipe bracket
Rollgabelschlüssel – adjustable wrench
rostig, verrostet – rusty
Rückwärtsgang – reverse gear

S

Sauerstoff – oxygen
schalldämpfende Füllung – silencer pads
schalten – change gear
Schalthebel – gear lever
Schaltplan – circuit diagram
Scheinwerfer – headlight
Schicht (Lage) – layer, coat
Schicht (Arbeitsabschnitt) – shift
Schiebedach-Rahmen – sunroof aperture panel
schlaff – slack
schleifen – grind, v
schleudern – skid, v
Schlichtfeile – finishing file
Schlitzschraubendreher – slotted screwdriver
schmieren; Schmiere – grease
schrauben; Schraube – screw
Schraubendreher – screwdriver
Schraubenschlüssel – spanner, wrench
Schraubstock – vice
Schraubstockbacken – vice jaw
Schrott – scrap
Schruppfeile – roughing file
Schub(-kraft) – motive power
Schutz – protection
Schutzblech – guard plate

Schutzbrille – goggles
Schutzkleidung – protective clothing
Schweißbrenner – welding torch
schweißen – weld, v
Schweißpistole – welding gun
Schwungrad – flywheel
Seitenblech – side (aperture) panel
Seitenschneider mit Handschutz – cutting nippers with hand guard
senken – countersink, v
Senkrechtschlitten – vertical slide
Sicherheit – safety
sicher stellen – ensure, v
Sicherung – fuse
Sitzkissen – cushion
Sitzschale, -wanne – seat pan
Sonnenblende – sunshade
Grad – grade
Spannung – voltage
sperren – lock, v
Sperrzone – restricted area
Spint – locker
Spiralbohrer – twist drill
Spritzwand – firewall
spülen – rinse
Stahl – steel
Stahlblech (Pressteil) – sheet metal
Stahlbürste – wire brush
Ständerbohrmaschine – column drill
Starter – starter motor
Steckeinsatz – socket
Steilheck – hatchback
stempeln – clock in, v
Steuerung – control
Stoßfängerträger – bumper bracket
Straßenverhältnisse – road conditions
Stromnetz – mains (electricity supply)
Stütze – bracket
synchronisiert – synchronized

T

Tablett – tray
Takt – stroke
Tauchbad – immersion bath
tauchen – dip, v
Teil, Bestandteil – component
Träger – member
Tuning (Motor) – tune-up
Türschweller – door sill

U

überwachen – monitor, v
umwandeln – convert, v
unbefestigte Straße – dirt road
undichte Stelle – leak
Unterboden – underbody
unterer Totpunkt – bottom dead centre (BDC)
Unterstellbock – jack stand
U-Stahl – section steel

V

Ventilfeder – valve spring
verbeult – dented
verbinden – join, v
Verbrauch – consumption
verbrauchen – consume, v
Verbrennungsmotor – internal combustion engine (ICE)
Verdichtungstakt – compression stroke
verkratzen – scratch, v
Verschleiß, Abnutzung – wear and tear
verstellbar – adjustable
Verunreinigung – contamination
Vielfachmessgerät für Volt und Ampere – multimeter
Vierradantrieb – four-wheel drive
vorbeugend – preventive
Vorderkotflügel – front wing, (US) fender
Vorderradantrieb – front-wheel drive
Vorrichtung, Gerät – device

W

Wagenheber – jack
Wählhebel – selector lever
Wechselstrom – alternating current (AC)
Werkbank – workbench
Werkstatt – workshop
Werkstattetage – shop floor
Werkzeug – tool
Werkzeugmaschine – machine tool
Windschutzscheibe – windscreen
Winkel – square
Winkelschleifer – angle grinder

Z

Zahnrad – cog-wheel
Zange – pliers
Zentralverriegelung – central locking
zünden – ignite, v
zünden (mit Zündaussetzern) – misfire, v
Zündkerze – spark plug
Zündung – ignition
zusammenbauen – assemble, v
Zusammenstoß – collision
Zylinderkopf – cylinder head

Umrechnungstabellen

1. Metrisches System

Längenmaße

1 millimetre (Millimeter) = 0.03937 inch
1 centimetre (Zentimeter) = 0.3937 inch
1 metre (Meter) = 39.37 inches
1 kilometre (Kilometer) = 0.6214 mile

Flächenmaße

1 square centimetre (Quadratzentimeter) = 0.155 square inch
1 square metre (Quadratmeter) = 10.764 square feet
1 square kilometre (Quadratkilometer) = 0.3861 square mile

Raummaße

1 cubic centimetre (Kubikzentimeter) = 0.061 cubic inch
1 cubic metre (Kubikmeter) = 35.315 cubic feet

Hohlmaße

1 litre (Liter) = 1.76 pints
= 0.22 gallon

Gewichte

1 kilogramme (Kilogramm) = 2.2046 pounds
1 metric ton (Tonne) = 0.9842 ton

2. Britisches System

Längenmaße

1 inch (Zoll) = 2,54 Zentimeter
1 foot (Fuß) = 30,48 Zentimeter
1 yard (Yard) = 91,44 Zentimeter
1 mile (Meile) = 1,609 Kilometer

Flächenmaße

1 square inch (Quadratzoll) = 6,45 cm^2
1 square mile (Quadratmeile) = 2,59 km^2

Raummaße

1 cubic inch (Kubikzoll) = 16,387 cm^3
1 register ton (Registertonne) = 2,832 m^3

Flüssigkeitsmaße

1 pint (Pinte) = 0,57 Liter
1 gallon (Gallone) = 4,546 Liter

Handelsgewichte

1 ounce (Unze) = 28,35 Gramm
1 pound (britisches Pfund) = 453,6 Gramm
= 0,453 Kilogramm
1 ton (Tonne) = 1016 Kilogramm

In den USA gilt großenteils dasselbe System wie in Großbritannien; einer der Hauptunterschiede ist das amerikanische Flüssigkeitsmaß gallon:
1 US gallon = 3,785 Liter

Mathematische Begriffe und Symbole

Addition:	2 + 3 = 5 (Two **plus** 3 **equals** five.)
Subtraction:	8 – 4 = 4 (Eight **minus** four **leaves** four.)
Multiplication:	9 x 4 = 36 (Nine **times** four **equals** thirty-six.)
Division:	55 : 11 = 5 (Fifty-five **divided** by eleven **equals** five.)

≠	does not equal
>	is more / greater than
<	is less than
°	degree
a two **by** four inch …	2 **auf** 4 Inches …

%	per cent
‰	per thousand

Quellenverzeichnis

Titelfoto	BMW AG, München
Seite 5	a, b, d, e: Hahn & Kolb, Stuttgart; c, g – j: Elmar Feuerbach, Remshalden; f: Robert Bosch GmbH, Stuttgart
Seite 6–7	Elmar Feuerbach, Remshalden
Seite 9	(oben von links nach rechts) Volkswagen AG, Wolfsburg; BMW AG, München; DaimlerChrysler AG, Sindelfingen; (unten links und Mitte) DaimlerChrysler AG, Stuttgart; (rechts) BMW AG, München
Seite 10	(oben) Elmar Feuerbach, Remshalden; (unten) Audi AG, Ingolstadt
Seite 11	Punch Library, London, UK
Seite 12	1: Elmar Feuerbach, Remshalden; 2–3: Hahn & Kolb, Stuttgart; 4: Elmar Feuerbach, Remshalden; 5: Bull Protect, Dietzenbach; 6: Hahn & Kolb, Stuttgart; 7: Kempel Berufskleidung GmbH, Bad Urach
Seite 13	(oben) DaimlerChrysler AG, Sindelfingen; (Mitte von links nach rechts) BMW AG, München; Citroën Deutschland AG, Köln; DaimlerChrysler AG, Sindelfingen; (unten links) BMW AG, München; (unten rechts) Audi AG, Ingolstadt; (unten) Volkswagen AG, Wolfsburg
Seite 14	(oben) Audi AG, Ingolstadt; (unten) Elmar Feuerbach, Remshalden
Seite 17	(oben links) Elmar Feuerbach, Remshalden; (oben rechts) Rothenberger Werkzeuge AG, Kelkheim; (unten) Audi AG, Ingolstadt
Seite 18	Elmar Feuerbach, Remshalden
Seite 19	Elmar Feuerbach, Remshalden
Seite 22	(oben) Elmar Feuerbach, Remshalden; (unten) Robert Bosch GmbH, Stuttgart
Seite 25	Elmar Feuerbach, Remshalden
Seite 26	(oben) Robert Bosch GmbH, Stuttgart; (unten) Elmar Feuerbach, Remshalden
Seite 28	Elmar Feuerbach, Remshalden
Seite 29	Citroën Deutschland AG, Köln
Seite 30	Graphik-Büro Böttcher & Bayer, Stuttgart
Seite 31	(links) Robert Bosch GmbH, Stuttgart; (Mitte und rechts) Adam Opel AG, Rüsselsheim
Seite 32	Elmar Feuerbach, Remshalden
Seite 33	(von links nach rechts) DaimlerChrysler AG, Stuttgart; (unten) Continental AG, Hannover
Seite 34	DaimlerChrysler AG, Stuttgart
Seite 37	(oben) DaimlerChrysler AG, Stuttgart; (unten) GETRAG Getriebe- und Zahnradfabrik Hermann Hagenmeyer GmbH & Cie KG, Untergruppenbach
Seite 39	(oben) Graphik-Büro Böttcher & Bayer, Stuttgart; (unten) DaimlerChrysler AG, Stuttgart
Seite 41	1: Jaguar Cars Ltd., Coventry, UK; 2–4: Citroën Deutschland AG, Köln
Seite 43	TÜV Süddeutschland, München
Seite 44	Elmar Feuerbach, Remshalden
Seite 45	Elmar Feuerbach, Remshalden; Klett-Archiv, Stuttgart
Seite 48	(oben) Dr. Ing. h.c. F. Porsche AG, Stuttgart; (unten links) Stojan Jović, Maichingen; (unten rechts) Dr. Manfred Semder, Besigheim